How to Make Your Customers Love You!

26 Ways to Make Customers Love You!

By

Kimberly Peters

Disclaimer

This publication is intended for use as an educational resource only and not as a blueprint for any specific application. Since all customers and businesses are different, it is up to the reader to determine the suitability of any or all parts of this publication as they pertain to their own individual situation. The writers, publishers and distributors of this book assume no responsibility for the use or application of any or all parts of this publication. The reader assumes totally responsibility for any use or application.

For More Books on

Customer Service Training,

Please go to our Website at:

http://www.infowhse.com

Contents

Introduction

When it comes to business, almost everything about a business is different from any other business. They might be larger or smaller, local or world-wide, have 1,000's of employees or just one or two. But when it comes to any business, there is one thing that every business has in common.

They all need customers.

Without customers there would be no one to purchase our products and services and no one to create the revenue to pay the owners and employees. There would be no money for product creation, inventory storage or any kind of research and development. So regardless of what kind of business you are in or how big or small your company might be, let's all agree that you need customers in order to survive.

But what if you are not a business but an employee? What do customers mean to you?

As we just said, customers provide businesses with the money they need to hire and pay for their salaries. So without customers you wouldn't have a job or any means to earn and income. Without an income you would not be able to pay for those little things in life like food, lodging, clothes and other things that we have come to need or rely on.

Though it might be hard to imagine after talking with some customers, the fact remains that customers are first and foremost people just like you and I. We all look for pretty much the same things in life and we tend to go to the sources where we stand the best chance of getting what we need or want with the best chances of success.

We also look to go through life by choosing the most positive alternatives to life's problems. In other words, we will go to great lengths to get what we want in life with as little trouble as possible. We will avoid negativity at every chance and search for ways to make our lives easier and better. So it makes sense that if these are the things we are looking for they are also the things our customers are looking for as well.

As you read this book you will probably find yourself nodding in agreement as you go from page to page.

That is because what we are going to read about is what makes customers happy. And if it makes your customers happy, it will probably make you happy as well.

Customer Service is nothing more than trying to give the customer more of what they need and want and less of what they don't need or want. In other words, customer service is about providing the very best customer experience for not just a few customers but for every single one. Though this is a huge simplification of an involved process, it sums it up very nicely.

This book is going to show you many ways to impress your customers and make them happy. As a business owner this is how you stay in business and grow your business. As an employee, this is how you show your customers that you care about them while at the same time increasing your value both in the marketplace and to your employer. No matter which side of the coin you may find yourself on, the information in this book will prove valuable to you.

Before we get started, there are a couple of things I would like to explain to you regarding this book.

First, there are two parts to this book. Part one deals with some basic attitudes and fundamentals of customer service. It is advisable for everyone to read this section first so that we are all on the same page as far as customer service and why certain things are important when it comes to our customers.

After that, the second section of this book contains all the ways we can help improve the customer experience and create customers who love us and our businesses. There is no particular order to these techniques or ideas because they all refer to different aspects of the customer experience. So feel free to skip around if there are certain things you feel are more important to you or to find things that may address a particularly urgent need.

Second, because some information might pertain to more than one tip or concept, you may find the same information repeated a couple of times throughout this book. This is not a copy error or an attempt to add pages to this book. Instead, it is designed to allow people to go from concept to concept in any order they desire and still have all the information they need to fully understand what we are talking about.

This will also help when it comes to retaining what you have read. Studies have shown that the more you hear or read something, the longer you will remember or retain it. Since most of the repeated information is among the most important or valuable information, repeating it is really a good thing.

That being said, the best way to learn from this book is to read it straight through from cover to cover.

If you want to skip around that's fine as well. But if you do skip around, do yourself a favor and re-read it from cover to cover as well. Not only will you retain the information better, you will probably also see some of it in a different light or from a different viewpoint.

Why Customer Service
is Important

Every day the business climate changes. Those who can adapt and keep pace survive. Those that don't, fail. This may seem like an over simplification, but it is true none the less.

Today's marketplace is growing at a rate that is unprecedented. The emergence of the Internet as a business resource has changed the way business is being done. Changed it in a way that will affect each and every business in the world today! Let's take a look at why this is so important.

It used to be that any business had a certain "territory" in which they did their business. This territory may have been shaped by the product or service the company provided, or by shipping and handling restrictions. The most common reason for limited territories was that it just was not possible to reach everyone in the world in a cost-effective manner.

These limited territories meant that each company had a limited amount of competition. Similar businesses within the area were known to their competition and each of these businesses could be monitored for their actions, sales, and other issues. In short, if you were "on the ball", you would not be taken by surprise by a competitor and your business placed at risk.

Because of this, a company may not be as aggressive when it comes to dealing with their customers. With limited competition, the options for their customers were also limited. If there are two companies selling a certain product or service in an area that means there are only two options for customers to obtain that product. Customers can go to either company, but they must choose one or the other.

When a customer has limited options, they may have to put up with a level of service that is less than they would like to see. In many areas, two businesses can survive quite nicely together with little competition between the two. When this is the case, there is little incentive to improve on the level of service they provide their customers. Since customer service costs money, there is little reason to spend money when their customer's options are so limited.

Enter A New Way of Doing Business!

Technology has given businesses a whole new way of reaching potential customers.

Small television stations have harnessed the power of satellites to put their signals into the homes of people all over the world. A once small station now has the power to reach a wide range of prospective customers!

Fax machines enable people to communicate much easier over their regular phone lines. Cell phones allow people to contact each other 24 hours a day, whether they are at home or on the road. Computers are available to manage inventory, create complex sales presentations, and reach people instantly through the use of e-mail! The options for businesses are growing by leaps and bounds! While this is certainly impressive, all this pales when compared to what is definitely the single most important business tool developed to date: The Internet!

The Internet enables businesses of all shapes and sizes to compete on an equal level no matter where they are located. This is a very important concept. This concept will forever change the way business is being done all over the world! Let's explore the impact of the Internet on business today.

The Internet & its Impact on Customer Service and Business

In the past, new and small businesses had to commit large sums of money and overhead in order to break through in their industry. Businesses had to start out in a small territory and gradually expand as their capital allowed. Big business had the resources to combat these small businesses and cause many of them to fail. Many a small business has failed because they couldn't compete with the "big boys"!

With the Internet, businesses of all shapes and sizes and placed before the public in an equal manner. When a person logs on to a website, they have no idea of what kind of company they are dealing with. The new company operating from a small office in a garage somewhere can have the same appearance as the established giant with the huge office complex! The content of the web site is what you see and what you base your decisions on.

Because of this, every business can compete in as large or small area as they desire! By placing their company products on the Internet, they can reach potential customers all over the world instead of just their "backyard"! Let's take a look at how that affects business in general.

A Whole New Set of Rules

With the arrival of the Internet, customers have an entire new source of businesses and resources available to them.

Now, instead of being limited to what is in their town or state, they can contact companies from around the world to buy their goods and services!

Let's take a look at what has changed for the consumer. Let's say that you want to buy a certain kind of power tool. Maybe it's an electric drill, saw, or other tool. In the past, you would go to the local tool or hardware center and buy it there. They may not have exactly what you want, or carry all the different models, but you would buy something that closely fit your needs. In some cases, you would look into the Yellow Pages for other stores close to your town. In most cases, you would visit each store and examine their selection and then return to the store that had what you wanted.

With the arrival of the Internet, you can contact manufacturers directly and buy over the Internet! You can use a search engine to find all kinds of sites that sell this particular product. There are even comparison sites that will give you a list of businesses that sell these tools and give you the prices! All without leaving your house! You can see everything available to you and buy something that fits your needs exactly, not something that just comes close!

You may be thinking that this manual is an advertisement for the Internet.

I assure you it is not. What we are trying to teach you is that with the advent of things like the Internet, the marketplace changes, and you must adapt your skills to meet these changes. Here is why technology has forced us to change the way we react and deal with people:

We have discussed the whole new set of resources available to consumers today. Since our customers have more options available to them, they are going to seek out and do business with the company or companies that make them feel the most appreciated and needed! When consumer options are limited, customers feel like they have to accept less. As consumer options increase, they feel entitled to be treated better and more fairly. They become more rigid in what they want, how they expect to be treated, and what they will and will not accept.

Because of these facts, and other facts you will discover later in this publication, Customer Service Skills will become the most valuable and most sought after skills in employees of virtually every industry and position today.

The Days of Ignorance Are Long Gone!

Another impact that the Internet has had on all kinds of consumers, businesses, and our population on the whole, is that it is extremely easy to get any kind of information.

Whenever a person wants to find out anything, they can search the Internet and come up with hundreds or thousands of potential sources of information.

How does that effect Customer Service you may wonder? When a customer comes wants to purchase a product or service, they will no longer take your word for the quality or exclusivity of your product. They will search and search until they get the information they require. Because of this, you must be honest and straightforward when it comes to talking about your company and its products. You cannot count on ignorance to get you through any more. Treat each customer like they are experts on your company and products.

Your customers are likely to become aware of your competition, too. Now that they are aware of additional resources available to them, you need to make sure you inform them of everything your company can offer that the competition can't. We'll get into this in detail a little later.

It is important for you to understand that people today are much more informed than they ever were before. Because of this, you must be prepared to deal with people on a whole other level. Make sure the information you give them is accurate and appropriate. Your credibility is at stake here. Be careful.

Why Customer Retention is Important

There are a lot of businesses and employees out there who seem to think that making customers happy is not that big of a deal. After all, if your products are good there will always be other customers who will walk in to take the place of the ones who leave. If your product is really popular, that might very well be true but it is still a dangerous view for any business owner or employee to take.

First of all, bringing a new customer through the front door or to a website for the first time is expensive. It requires advertising, marketing, sales expertise and quite a bit of hand-holding. New customers need to establish a certain level of trust in a business before they actually purchase. You might have to talk to that customer 5 or 6 times before they purchase from you.

Established customers, on the other hand, already know about you and your business. If you have treated them well and given them a great experience before, they will walk through the doors in the future to buy more from you. There will be very little need to establish a level of trust because that has already been accomplished, In fact, you might be interested to know that repeat customer usually buy more than new customers. Their sales are usually larger and they purchase more frequently once they become comfortable with you and your business.

Established customers also don't require nearly as much marketing or promotional resources. After all, they already know about your business and have used your products and services. If they were happy, they will not need to see a commercial or read an ad to get them to come back. They will come back because they has a positive experience before. That is far more effective than any ad or commercial.

Studies have shown that it can cost up to 10 times MORE to bring a new customer through the doors as it takes to keep an existing one happy. You do not have to be an accountant to see that keeping existing customers happy is much more cost effective and less stressful than having to replace those same customers every month or year.

Another reason for keeping existing customers happy is that we need people to come back again and again because that is where our businesses get their stability from. Repeat customers provide business and income on a regular basis. These are the people we can count on and help keep our expenses to a minimum. The more people we keep happy, the more profitable our businesses will become.

We also want to keep existing customers happy because no matter how great a business might be, there will always be a percentage of customers who are not coming back next year. This might have nothing to do with the business or the products and services but rather their need for those products and services.

For example, if you sell toys, then parents will stop needing those toys when their kids are grown. Until their need is renewed by grandchildren or other young people, they will not come back that often. They could love you and your business but they no longer need what you are selling.

Then there are those loyal customers who move from the area and away from your business. Unless your business also sells on the internet they will probably look for stores or sources closer to where they live now. Even internet businesses may lose customer when people move because their new location has a local source for the same products.

On the more morbid side, every customer, no matter how loyal, is eventually going to pass away and with them go their business. Depending on the type of products and service you sell this may be a big deal or a minor one. If you sell toys you wouldn't worry so much but if you sell senior citizen health care products this could be a huge factor for your business.

Let's shift gears once again and talk about something that might really bring the need to retain customers into focus for you.

Did you ever think about what happens when a customer stops doing business with your company? Do you think they just stop using the product or service because they don't get it from you anymore? They don't stop using the product unless they no longer have a need for it. But if they need it and don't want to buy it from you anymore, what do you think happens?

Those customers move over to your competition. So every customer you lose becomes a customer your competition gains. More important they gain it without a lot of advertising expense or other costs. You provided your customer with a reason to look elsewhere and they wound up at your competition.

Everything in this book is aimed towards not giving any customer a reason to look elsewhere.

Instead, we are going to try and give them reason after reason to stay with your business and not to even think about looking anywhere else. We want to create an impression in your customer's mind that there is no better place to go for the product and services you offer.

Because the first time a sliver of doubt gets into their heads this is when they start looking elsewhere. And when they walk into your competition's store and they see someone who is a new customer, they will give them their best and you will have lost a customer at their expense.

So let's just do our best to make sure that never happens.

Who Needs to Be Trained in Customer Service?

Another misconception when it comes to employees and employers alike is exactly who really needs to be trained in customer service. The common view is that only those people who come in direct contact with customers need this critical training. But those of us who truly understand the entire customer experience know the right answer.

It sometimes helps to view the entire customer experience from the first time they walk through the doors until the experience is complete as a chain with a series of links. Each link will represent one phase or part of the customer experience. If any of these links should be a weak spot or a complete failure the entire customer experience can break or fail.

Here are a couple of examples. You tell me whether each experience would be perceived as a positive or negative experience.

A customer walks through the door and is treated very rudely by the salesman or even totally ignored. He has questions that are left unanswered and he walks out because he isn't sure what to buy.

A customer walks through the door, is treated perfectly by the salesman, they find the perfect product but unfortunately the product is out of stock and the customer needs it today.

A customer walks through the door, is treated great by the salesman and they find the perfect product. He purchases it on credit and takes it home. But then a month later he gets a bill for the wrong price and a higher interest rate.

A customer walks through the door, finds a very helpful salesman, finds the perfect product and purchases it. The delivery people miss the first appointment and it has to be rescheduled. Meanwhile the customer had taken the afternoon off because you do not deliver nights or weekends. To make matters even worse, when they unboxed the product it was damaged and will need to be replaced.

We could go on and on with examples but what did you notice when you read all the examples? All the examples above were examples of a negative customer experience.

Something along the way was done wrong or not at all. In each example the customer was left feeling negative about the final customer experience.

The other thing that is in common with each example is that certain parts of the experience went well but one other thing went wrong or was not done to the satisfaction of the customer. So even though 90% of what happened was positive, the overall experience was negative.

Those were the two easy things to spot but there was one more common factor in every example except for the first one.

The first example had the blame placed on the salesman who is a common part of the customer service experience. The sales man is the person who meets the customer face to face or talks to them over the phone and helps them get what they need or want. In the beginning, the salesperson has a huge input on the direction in which the customer experience goes. If the salesman is not a positive factor the customer will often walk out. So it is critical that the salesman, or whoever might make the first contact with the customer, be trained in proper customer service techniques.

I am sure we can all agree on that because the salespeople, and others who have direct contact throughout the sales process need to know how to properly interact with the customer.

But in each of the other experiences, the "problems" were not caused by any of the sales people or any person that had a part in the sales process. In all the other examples, the mistakes or errors were made by people who are behind the scenes. These are the people we never meet, and usually don't talk to, unless there is a problem.

We are talking about people in the billing department, the people who are in charge of inventory and the people who deliver, install or repair the products. If any of these people make a mistake, it might wipe out any goodwill or positive impression that was generated up to that point. With that in mind, I am sure you see the benefit in having every employee in the company properly trained in customer service.

It is important to realize this because many businesses and employees are under the impression that only a select few people need to learn these skills and techniques. But from what you just read, it should be clear that no matter what your function might be within a company, you MUST understand the customer and the impact on what your part of the customer experience is.

So the answer to the question of who need to be trained is everyone. The training isn't expensive and it doesn't take long either. There is no excuses for anyone, whether it is the owner of the business or any employee, not to get these skills. That is what we talk about throughout this book.

We urge everyone who reads this book to learn as much as they can when it comes to customer service and the customer experience. Even if you don't think you need these skills get them anyway because the truth is, you need them just like the sales people and the cashiers and other people. Trust me when I tell you that no matter what your role in the company might be, you can either be a positive or negative influence on the entire customer experience.

It's your choice and it should be an easy one.

What is the REAL Value
of a Customer?

Good customer service doesn't have to cost money. In fact, it has been shown that customer service skills can actually save a company money in the long run. Studies have shown that it can cost 5 - 10 times more to get a new customer than it does to keep an existing one happy! Let's talk about that for a moment.

Think about what has to happen for a customer to change from another company or product to your company. Your company has to prove to that customer that you can produce a better product, or do something better than the company that person is using now. How do you do that? You accomplish this by trying to alter that person's perception of your company. Several common ways to accomplish this are:

Hiring of sales people to go out and solicit sales. Create media advertising to showcase your products and services. Get exposure for your product in trade publications. Create promotional campaigns to promote your products and services.

All of the above cost money. A lot of money! The sole focus of the above is to bring new customers to your company. Companies need new customers in order to grow or even stay the same. Every year, a certain percentage of existing customers will leave your company no matter what you do. Some will die, some will move out of your area, and some will no longer have a use for your products. In order for your company to remain in business, you must have a steady stream of customer to replace the one that leave.

If you lose customers due to poor service, this increase the number of new customer you must bring in. This places an enormous burden on the company. Existing customers already know what you can do for them. They already found something in your company that they like. That gives you an incredible advantage. Don't provide an excuse to send your customer to your competition. Keep your customer service satisfaction rating high. Involve your customers in your business and follow their suggestions.

Keeping your existing customers just makes good business sense. You've worked hard to get them. Now work even harder to keep them. Think of your existing customers as an army of unpaid salespeople!

People that will pass on their good experiences to those that may also need the products and service your company can provide! The other side of the coin is also true. Your customers can also relay tales of unpleasant experiences, which can drive customer straight to your competition. Take care of your customer's every day and keep them on your side!

How Much are your Customers Worth?

When you think about your customers, how much do you think they are worth to your company? If someone buys $100.00 worth of product from your company then that customer is worth $100.00, right? Not necessarily! That customer could be worth much more!

It is important to know the real worth of a customer because the human mind tends to react differently to things of different value. For example, if you buy something for $5.00 and it breaks two months later, you would probably throw it out and buy another one. If you purchased something for $500.00 and it broke two months later, you would have a totally different reaction. You would demand repair or replacement and would expend whatever efforts required to accomplish that.

The same would hold true for treating your customers. You would treat a customer better if they represented a larger value to the company. You may feel you treat everyone the same but the amount of business a company does with a customer is bound to influence these decisions.

The value of a customer includes the value of his or her recent purchases, recurring purchases, and the amount of business that customer represents in the future. These are concrete values. Other things that should be taken into consideration would include the customer's ability to influence other people to do business with your company, word of mouth advertising, and the industry in which the customer is involved. (Can the customer help you obtain additional business within the customers industry?)

Here's an example:

A customer walks into a deli and buys a sandwich for $4.00 and a drink for $1.00. He goes back to his office and finds the sandwich is full of poor quality meat with lots of fat in it. He goes back to the deli and demands a new sandwich. The deli owner refuses and an argument starts. The deli owner says to himself; "This guy only spent 5 bucks. This argument is just not worth my time. Let him go somewhere else." He tells the guy to leave the deli.

What did the deli owner lose? The sandwich cost him $2.00 to make so he saved $2.00. He did lose a customer but that was only $5.00 so no big deal.

Wrong! Let's look at things a different way. This customer eats lunch out twice a week. That's $10.00 per week or $520.00 per year. He also eats in an office with 20 other people that also eat out twice a week. He goes back and tells them how he was treated. Two more people decide they don't like that kind of treatment so they don't go back. That's $520 X 2 or $1020.00 more lost. So far the deli owner lost $1560.00! The customer then finds a new deli that is looking to add customers. Their sandwiches are bigger and their prices are better. It's a bit of a drive but the switch off going so that one person is making the trip. Eventually the other people in the office see the bigger and better sandwiches and 5 more people switch. That's $520 X 5 or $2600.00. The deli owner has now lost $3620.00 all because he chose to save $2.00 on replacing a sandwich! What was the value of that customer? Was it $5.00 or $3620.00? Do you think the deli owner would have treated this customer just a little bit different if he had realized this customer's true value?

You may think this is funny or just plain outrageous but it can happen. I personally know a gentleman that owned an electronic repair business. One of his major accounts was a string of video stores.

One store manager made an unreasonable request and this gentleman refused to honor the request because it would mean $100.00 loss for something that was not his fault. The store manager found someone else to do his store repairs and eventually the new business took all the stores in that chain away. It can and does happen. Don't let it happen to you!

In the case of the deli above, who knows what other business may have been lost? Maybe the owner of the company would like to have some company meetings catered. Who do you think will get that business? There are also employee businesses such as Christenings, graduations, etc. that may require catering. All this needs to be figured into the equation.

In the case of service businesses, we must figure in the cost of service contracts, maintenance contracts, equipment purchases, life span of equipment, and one more big item: supplies. Supplies are important because they represent on-going or recurring revenue. The customer may buy a machine every five years but they will buy supplies every month. In most cases the profit on supplies is where the money is made! All these things must be considered when trying to establish the true value of the customer.

The next time you are talking with a customer, place a large value on him and see if you are willing to go the extra mile for him the. I think you will be surprised how your attitude will change!

Why You Need to Be Pro-Active

There are two ways we can handle almost any situation in life. We can take control of the situation before it gets more serious or out of hand or we can let the situation dictate how we react and what we do. Almost always we will have a better result when we take control of things and do them on our terms and schedule.

This is called being pro-active. Being pro-active means addressing things before you need to or at least in the very beginning. Another way of looking at it would be taking care of problems before they become problems. This is usually the best way to go.

An example of being pro-active is not only resolving issues once you have become aware of them but also by taking a closer look of things and taking action before someone complains. That means looking for things that might or could become problems and making the necessary changes or adjustment to eliminate the problem before it gets started.

This is important because customers sometimes will not give you a second chance. If they have a negative experience, they will not go back again to make sure it was a fluke. Instead, they will search elsewhere never to return. The only time they may come back is if they had a positive experience before or if your business was recommended by someone they respect or trust. Even then you might or might not get a second chance.

The fact is, customers don't really care why something negative or bad happened. They only care that it happened. They also don't care about your rule, processes or procedures. Those things are your problems not theirs. If there is something about your business that turns them off, they will just leave. If there is something they don't like about the way you treated or interacted with them, they will either leave or request someone else in the future.

Customers do this simply because they usually can. Unless you sell a product that only you are selling, then they will simply search for another source and purchase it there. If the experience is bad enough, and you are the only source for that product, they might go as far as trying to search for another product even if it is not as good or more expensive.

Another reason you need to be pro-active is that you should NEVER give your customers the slightest reason to look elsewhere.

Maybe there is another store or source that provides greater value or superior service or product selection. Maybe it is one of those "big box" retailers that you could never hope to under-cut or beat their selection. Whatever the situation might be, if your customers are not aware that they exist then you might keep them as customers. But if you give them a reason to check other places, that might be the end of your customer.

As if all of those reasons aren't enough, think about another aspect of a dissatisfied customer or someone who has a negative impression or opinion of your business. What do angry people usually do when they feel wronged or taken advantage of? They tell other people. They might tell co-workers or friends and today, they might go to an online forum and tell hundreds, thousands, or millions about their experience.

When this happens their comments do not have to be true in order to hurt your business. All those comments need to be effective and cause damage is to be somewhat believable. Because if someone else believes them to be true then they are true whether they really are or not. That is because, fair or not, their perception also becomes their version of reality in their minds and they will react according to what they believe to be true.

Here is something else to consider:

Studies have shown that it can take as many as 10 positive experiences to overcome the effects of just one negative experience. So if your customer does give you the benefit of the doubt and give you another try, you just don't have to satisfy them once or twice to restore their faith, you might have to hit a home run the next 10 times they purchase from you!

If any of those 10 times result in another negative experience, you might have totally lost the ability to ever win that customer back again! So with all of this in mind, I hope you see that the importance of not only resolving issues and problems quickly, but the value in eliminating the causes of those negative experiences before they happen again.

The question now should be not whether or not there are problems that need addressing but rather how you can discover potential problems now and fix them before any customers are impacted. Fortunately, there are a few things you can do both as a business owner or employee to help make this happen.

First, try and look at everything in your job or business from the customer's point of view. Sometimes this can be difficult because you are used to seeing things from the business point of view. But look at every rule, policy, process and procedure and ask yourself "Does this make things easier or more difficult for my customer?"

If the answer is that it makes things easier then you are good to go. But if anything makes something harder or less positive in the eyes of the customer, you should take steps to change things to make them more customer friendly. Anything you can do to make it easier and more pleasant to shop in your store will make more of your customers happy.

But that is not to say that you should place your business at risk either. There needs to be checks and balances within your business to protect it as well. After all, if you do everything to make your customer happy and it causes you to go out of business, then you are out of business and the customer has nowhere to go for their products and services in the future.

So what we need to do is look at everything from both sides. Look at it from the customer's point of view first to see what can be made better or easier for the customer. Ask yourself what would make the customer want to do business with you instead of someone or somewhere else? Then, once you know what needs to happen, take a look at it from the business point of view to see what is practical and advisable.

For example, it would be wonderful if you sold everything with a lifetime guarantee.

Your customers would love it because they could use something for 20 years and then get their money back when it broke. But your business could not possibly stand that exposure if the manufacturer did not provide the same warranty. So a lifetime warranty would be out.

But maybe your current 30 day return policy is too restrictive especially if other businesses offer 60 or 90 days. IN that case, maybe changing your policy to 90 or 120 days would make your business more attractive while also limiting your exposure and costs. In this case both the business and the customer would emerge as winners.

Go through everything, no matter how trivial or small the item might be and identify potential action items or problems that need to be addressed. Tackle the major ones first. But that I mean if you have two things to change and one would affect all your customers while the other would affect just 10% of the customers, do the one that effects everyone first and then handle the other one. Do first what gives you the most reward when it comes to how the customer feels about your business.

Another way to identify potential problems or areas of improvement is to ask your customers. Have a suggestion box or survey your customers to find out what they liked or didn't like about you and your business. Don't just ask what they liked, find out what they didn't like as well. That is just as important and sometimes even more important.

Knowing what your customers like and dislike about your business or yourself personally will give you an idea of what you need to change. Keep in mind that it is not up to the customer to change to suit your expectations but rather the other way around. You need your customers to purchase from you instead of your competition. If they stop buying, you stop selling.

And when that happens, we all know what happens next.

The Shocking Eye-Popping Truth!

One of the things most businesses and employees don't realize is that something most of our customers don't do can place our businesses and sometimes our careers in jeopardy. What our customers don't usually do is tell us why they are leaving before they leave.

It might surprise anyone in customer service that this is true because we have all dealt with more than our fair share of angry customer. Most of those angry customers seem to have absolutely no problem explaining in very raised voices exactly what their concerns and complaints are. But as crazy as this might seem, the majority of customers who experience a negative situation just walk out the door and never return.

Now it might seem that this is a kind of blessing. Chances are those angry people who yell and scream at us aren't going to come back either so if the result is the same shouldn't we be happy that they don't take the time to yell and scream at us?

Actually, we shouldn't be happy at all.

Though it is not pleasant to stand or sit there and listen to someone yell and scream or make outrageous demands, at least we have the opportunity to listen to them and determine what their problem or thoughts really are. Even if those feelings or problems are not legitimate, we do get to understand how our customer's come to thank about our business.

When someone walks out the door never to return, we often have no idea why they left. That means that if problems really do exist, we still might not know what those problems are. We might try to guess and waste time and resources trying to fix something that really isn't broken. When that happen ono one benefits. In fact, everyone loses.

When someone stops and tells us why they leave we at least know why and we can see if their complaints are justified. If they are justified then we have the ability to take corrective action to make sure this doesn't happen again in the future. If the customer is just being unreasonable, we might come to the conclusion that there was nothing really wrong and that the customer was the problem.

But even when the customers are the problem, that still means that you lost a customer.

So maybe even though the customer's demands or expectations were unreasonable, you still would have the opportunity to make something just a little bit better so that even fewer people might come to the same conclusion. It is usually more difficult to deal with perception issues than it is to fix legitimate and actual problems.

We are telling you this to reinforce just how important it is to survey your customers and find other ways to solicit the opinions of all your customers. If you do that effectively you can keep ahead of the issues and resolve most of them before something causes you to lose another customer.

Sometimes this could be as simple as having someone by the door to talk to people on their way out. Maybe they would just ask if they found everything they needed or some other open ended question designed to give the customer as easy way to voice their feelings at that moment.

This is important because many people do not want to bring attention to themselves and might even feel a little intimidated by the people in the store. But when someone else starts the dialogue and asks for their opinions or thoughts, they just might share them. But sometimes there is an even better way to handle these situations.

What if part of the customer experience was designed to illicit these comments during the customer experience itself?

What is people were to ask if you needed any help or if you had found everything you needed? What if people offered assistance before having to ask for it?

This is often effective because there are customers who will never ask for help or assistance. Instead, they will look around and if they don't find what they needed they will just leave and go look somewhere else. When that happens it makes no difference if that product was in some other area of the store or website or if it was in the warehouse because it did not make it out to the sales floor yet. When people don't find what they want and don't ask for it, you lose a sale and possibly a customer.

Never take customers for granted or believe that they will voice their displeasure or tell you when something goes wrong. Because while some will tell you there are a lot of others who will just walk out without saying a word. That is wonderful for your competition but bad for you and your business.

So solicit information and feedback for your customers and then be prepared to act on it whenever it is necessary. That is the way we keep our fingers on the pulse of what our customers are thinking and feeling when it comes to our business.

Making Everyone Winners!

Let's get one thing clear right from the start. Customer service and interaction with a customer is not a competition or contest. The process is not something where someone comes out victorious. We need to understand that whenever someone is a winner that means that someone else, or other people, come out as the losers. Since no one wants to feel like they lost, we should do our best to avoid "the winner take all" mentality.

When it comes to interacting with customer we need to change the way we approach selling and customer relations. Instead of looking for winners and losers, we need to instead search for "win-win" resolutions where both the business and the customer gets the most of what they are looking for.

That means looking at things from the customer point of view and trying to figure out ways of giving the customer as much of what they want as possible while still protecting the business at the same time. At times this might require some out of the box thinking.

Customers come back when they feel they got an exceptional value not just a decent value. In order to make an impression, propel must get something very different from what they expected. If they expected to pay a fair price and your price was fair, they will not be impressed. But if they expected to pay a fair price and your price was much lowering THAT makes a great impression in the mind of the customer.

But the impression doesn't always revolve around price. In fact, it may be surprising to know that price is not usually the most important factor when deciding what or where to purchase. Even more important than price is the OVERALL value that your customer gets by doing business with you or your company.

You can achieve a win-win outcome when you think of ways to increase the perceived value of the purchase in the eyes of the customer. Trying things called "value added extras" can really make a big impression while not costing you much of anything to provide.

That is why so many companies use things like free delivery, longer hours, greater convenience, larger selection and other things to help create the image of getting a much better overall value by purchasing through you. It is not so much the actual value but what the customer perceives that really matters.

For example, a customer might place a high value on convenience because their schedule is so busy that they do not have the time to go from store to store to find everything they need. So if your business has the reputation of having the best selection then that has a high value for that customer.

If someone works 6 days a week from 9AM-5PM then evening or Sunday hours would have a high value as well. If you offered evening or Sunday delivery that would be a high value extra because the customer could be there for delivery without having to take time off of work. Again, it is not so much the cost to you for providing something to the customer it is the value they attach to that "extra".

One of the keys to making customers really love you is being able to identify what is really important to them and then providing that to them in the best way possible. The only way for you to be successful in doing this is to understand your customer base and designing your business around their needs or demands.

One way of accomplishing this is by asking your customers what they would like to see you offer to them when they become customers. You will be surprised when not everyone says lower prices. Although some customers will mention price, other customers will make comments about what you stock, the service you provide and other things that might be important to them.

They really great thing is that whenever one customer mentions something that they would place a high value on, other customers are bound to feel the same way. After all we are all people deep down and we all want pretty much the same things in life. So if something is in demand by one customer, chances are it will be appreciated by others as well.

Another way of trying to figure out how to increase the value without lowering the price is to ask yourself if you have something that will either make the customers life better, easier, or faster. If you can hit one or two of those items you will make more customers happy. If you can hit a home run and hit all 3, you really would have a winner on your hands!

Think about that for a moment. Same day delivery is a great thing because it gets the product into the hands of the customer faster. If the purchase is something important like a refrigerator or washing machine that could be huge. That alone could bring a sale to you over somewhere else.

If someone came into the store looking for a certain product and you could show them a model that would accomplish the same thing in less time with less work, your customer would definitely appreciate that.

That is the difference between giving people what they asked for and giving them something better. Anyone can sell a customer something they specifically ask for. But the business who thinks about how to make things better will better serve the customer!

Be Positive!

Before we get to the 26 ways to make customers love you, let's discuss one of the main things you should keep in mind whenever you deal with customers. It's a really easy thing to do but you would be surprised how many people fail to follow this one simple process.

Whenever you interact with customers, always adopt a positive tone and speech pattern. Avoid negative words like can't or won't. Your customers don't care about what you can't do, they want to hear about what you can do for them. They also don't care about your policies and procedures either. So when you talk to customers, concentrate on the positive and avoid negative sounding words.

Another problem with negative words is that sometimes when we hear a negative word our brains shut down and we fail to hear the rest of what is being said. All we heard was something negative and that probably meant that we weren't getting something we wanted or that something was not going our way.

So instead of telling a customer you cannot do something, focus on what you can do for them and tell them that. If you cannot offer a free replacement, tell them you can do a warranty repair at no charge or give them a discount if it is just out of warranty.

Instead of telling them what the lower model cannot do, instead tell them what the better model can do. Instead of saying "This model =cannot do that" say instead "If you need to handle heavier loads we have this model her which can do that for you." This way you are not putting down the lower model which might be all the customer can afford.

Don't waste time on what the manufacturer cannot or will not do, instead concentrate on the options open to the customer.

For example, if a customer demands a free replacement of a one year old product but the manufacturers doesn't cover that. Instead of telling them you cannot do that, instead tell them you can arrange to have their unit shipped out or repaired free of charge. If a loaner product is available offer that as well. The customer might be accepting of that if you present in a positive manner.

The other benefit of being positive is that the customer listens to you and hears all about how you want to help them resolve their issues. You don't tell them "no" you offer solutions.

You show them that you want to help them resolve their problems and that you want to be part of that process.

By being positive you are showing them that you want to be part of the solution not part of the problem.

This can also help calm people down and make them easier to deal with. Being seen as an ally instead of an enemy can make negotiations go faster and easier. You will find out that people usually respond more favorably to people that have positive outlooks and approaches than they do to negative people.

Customer service is so much about perception and positive people help form a much more positive impression on customers as well. You might not be able to give the customers what they want but you will make them feel much better about it if you offer alternatives or options to them in the process.

You should also use the positive approach when it comes to giving the customer reasons for them to do business with you rather than your competition. No one like to hear someone put another person or business down. A lot of customers will be turned off by that.

But those same customers need to know about what you offer so if you give them the advantages without putting down your competition that will help you get your point across in a more positive manner.

For example, if you offer free delivery and your competition doesn't you could say "Jim's Appliance doesn't offer free delivery but we do. We are a much better value than buying from Jim's." That could come off as a negative statement to some customers.

But you could also say "If you need that delivered we offer free delivery which is something that makes buying from us a much better value." That is a totally positive statement that showcases a benefit that has value to the customer. That is a much better way of getting the same point across to the customer.

To help you get started with changing to a more positive approach, start out by changing all your negative words to positive ones. Concentrate on what you can do and not what you cannot do. When talking about products talk about what the product can do and not what it cannot do. Just keep it positive at all times and you will be fine.

Are we positive about that?

Now, here are

26 Ways You
Can Make Your
Customers Love You!

1. Make Their Lives Easier

As a rule anything you can do to make life and shopping easier on your customers will be appreciated by every customer. Life is hectic these days and if there are ways to get in and out faster with the same results your customers will love you for it.

There are several ways you can make things easier for your customers. While you don't have to do all of these things in order to make your customers love you, the more you do the better off you will be!

Have a good selection of the type of products that you sell so they customer will be able to purchase what they came in for. Have several models for them to choose from so they can get more of what they want from you rather than anyone else. Stock as many type of parts and accessories as well so you can become the one stop source for everything they need when it comes to the types of products you sell. After all, if they have to go somewhere else to get an accessory or replacement part, why not just buy from that store in the first place?

Make things easy to find. That means making your store or website easy to navigate and arrange things in an orderly and reasonable way. That means placing like products and accessories near each other in the store or on the website.

This not only makes things easier to find but should increase sales as people will see related products either on the way to what they want or on the way back to the cashier. These extra purchases are called "impulse buys" and they only occur when you make it easy for the customer to find or see those products.

Streamline your purchase processes as well. If you own a retail store, make sure you have enough cashiers to handle checkouts so there are no long lines. People sometimes will pick out what they need and then leave it all in the cart if they see 5 or 10 people in line ahead of them. For many people time is money and long lines are definitely a turn off.

If you own a brick and mortar store, make it easy to get to and have hours that make your store very convenient for everyone. This might mean evening and weekend hours and perhaps even a holiday or two. People are usually willing to pay a little more for a lot more convenience. This also applies to support services like repairs and deliveries. If you customer doesn't have to rearrange their schedule or take time off from work, they will appreciate that. Have plenty of parking available as well so people will not worry about getting a parking spot. People will go somewhere else if parking is perceived to be a hassle.

Streamline the return / exchange process to make it easier and faster. These tasks are perceived as negative experiences in the first place because you are either dissatisfied with the product or it is the wrong model or size. So you have to go to the store yet again and when you walk out you do not have anything new or exciting to show for it. You have what you had when you walked in or you have less if you did a return.

Make your return policies liberal so the customer has more than a reasonable amount of time to return something. Offer money back and not just a store credit. Doing so will make your business more desirable for purchases when they know they will not just get a store credit but can get their cash back.

All of these things by themselves are minor things. But every one of them has the ability to either positively or negatively contribute to the overall perception of you and your business. If getting to your business or if purchasing from your business is perceived to be a real hassle, it will scare some people away. If shopping at your business is perceived to be a pleasant and positive experience, you will attract more customers from other sources as well as making your existing customers happy.

If you think that doing any or all of these things will cost too much money, this might change your mind.

People are almost always willing to pay a little bit more for a lot of convenience and a positive experience. The opposite is also true. If your business is a hassle to get to or purchase from, you are going to have to offer REALLY low prices in order to compensate your customer for the hassles involved.

So not only does making life easier for your customers help bring more people through your doors or to your website, it also will help them purchase more products and may even result in your ability to charge slightly higher prices. But if you combine lower prices with added convenience, expansion might just be in your future!

2   Give Them More than they Expect

When someone walks into your business to make a purchase, they have a certain expectation in mind. They have an idea of what they expect to find as far as selection, price and atmosphere is concerned. If you give people what they expect, well, that is what they expect to get. You will not make much of an impression on your customers when you give them what they expect.

But if you give them MORE than what they expect, that is where the magic happens. If they walk through your stores and expect to see 3 or 4 different models and you have 30 different models that will impress them. If they expect to pay $100 for their product and your price is $59.95 or $69.95 that will impress them. If they expect a salesman to push the most expensive products or spend just a few seconds with them but your salesman spends time figuring out what they really need and gets them the perfect product that will impress them!

You don't hear people tell their friends "I went to Herb's Appliance and they had exactly what I thought they would have!" What does that mean? Did you expect a large selection or small selection? Did you expect high prices or low prices? No one raves to anyone when they got what they expected.

But you will hear people say things like "I went to Herb's Appliance last night and that place was amazing. I thought they would have 4 or 5 washers but they had over 20! And their salesman gave us the perfect model for our needs and the prices was, like, $100 less than what we thought it would be!"

Which one of those customers do you think was really impressed with that store? Which comment would make you want to go to that same store the next time you needed a similar product or other product that business sold? Chances are it would be the store that someone raved about.

People remember anything that is different than what they expected. This works for both positive and negative experiences. If something really good or bad happens, you will remember it. But if something so-so happens, chances are you will forget about it in a short time. It will not make an impression on you.

So instead of trying to meet the expectations of the customer, instead try to blow them away. Make them stop dead in their tracks and wonder what the heck is going on. Make them wonder how you can make such a great offer or provide such a huge selection. Try and really make an impression.

If they walk in expecting A & B, don't just give them A & B, throw in C, D & E as well. If they expect delivery in 3 or 4 days, get it them the same day or the next day. If you can do this with most of your customers you will not only make them happy, you will close more sales as well.

Many customers have a problem deciding on what they want to purchase. The will leave and think about it some, let some times pass to make sure that is what they want and they will often shop around to make sure they are getting a good deal. But what sometimes happens is that they walk into another store and get the same deal or value that you offered, they might realize this is a good deal but since they are in the other place already, they might just buy it there instead of with you!

But when you give a customer more than they expect, when you blow them away with what they perceive as a great or overwhelming offer, they will be far more likely to purchase right then and there and not be tempted to give it some time or check elsewhere for a better deal.

Also consider that the best overall deal or value is not just about price. It includes other value added services such as free delivery and other add-ons which may cost you little or nothing but have a huge perceived value to the customer.

Things like longer warranties or free set up in the home might be enough to close the sale without costing you very much at all.

We said it already and we will say it again, it is not what it costs you that matters. It is the value the customer places on something that can make all the difference.

So put together the best package you possibly can and give every customer the most or best value they can get and you will find more and more people flocking to you and your business than you ever thought possible.

All because you made a positive impression that your customers will not forget!

3   Be Empathetic

Remember when we said that customers are people just like you and I? Well, if we believe that to be true, then we should understand that they will probably be looking for the same things that you and I look for in a given situation.

So when you have a problem, what are you looking for?

Are you looking for someone who appears to have zero interest in you or your problems or would you like someone who makes you feel that they have an honest desire to help you resolve your problems?

If you are like 99.9% of people you would choose the person who appears to really want to help you solve your problems. That is because somewhere in our minds we will feel that we have a better chance of getting the best possible resolution from someone who appears to care about us and our problems.

That is why a person's ability to show empathy is so important. Empathy is being able to make someone feel that you care about them and their problems or needs. Empathy means acknowledging their problems and letting them know that you want to help them resolve those problems.

Please understand that acknowledging a problem is NOT the same as taking responsibility for it. That is a big difference and one that you must understand so that you can express empathy with the right words and phrasing so you do not lead the customer to think that you are telling then the problem is your fault.

For example, if someone comes in with a problem that they caused themselves and is not a defect you might say something like "I'm sorry that you are having a problem. Let's see what I can do to help resolve this." That tells the customer you want to help but it does not say you are accepting responsibility for the problem only that you want to help resolve it.

Now if you were to say something like "I'm sorry you have this problem and I will do whatever it takes to fix it" the customer might infer from that statement that you are accepting responsibility for the problem no matter what the root cause might have been. Those particular words could come back to haunt you and cause you problems especially if the issue escalates into a legal situation.

In some cases, especially when the customer caused the problem, your help might be just explaining what caused the problem to the customer. If they broke the product by abusing it or by using it in ways that it was not intended, you might explain that to them.

You would not necessarily replace the product because it was not defective but you would still try to help them.

If you assumed responsibility for the problem you might wind up having to repair or replace the product because that is what your words inferred. So express empathy but not responsibility.

Show that you care and that you honestly want to help a customer either resolve their problem or to help assist them in getting the right solution for that problem. You can go the extra mile if you feel it is appropriate and that will help the customer love you even more.

But just taking the time and making the customer feel that you have their problems and best interests in mind will go a long way towards making the customer feel more comfortable and more secure during the conversation. Just be careful in your word because some customers just love to twist and turn you words and use them against you in the future.

If you are in your own business then you can set the rules as to what your employees should be saying to their customers. If you are an employee, talk to your owner or manager to see how you should talk to the customer. If they are not aware of the concept of empathy, nicely explain it to them. Then find out what you should say and how you should say it so both you and your customer can have a better relationship.

4   Be Responsive

Customers like people who take action and help them either choose their products, help them through the purchase process or help them resolve their problems. They want someone who is going to follow through on what they said they would do. What they don't want are people who say all the right things but never back them up.

As someone charged with making customers happy that means always following through on what you say you will do. Not just someone of the time or most of the time but ALL of the time. Anything less will place the relationship of the customer and the business at risk.

For example, if you say you are going to talk to the owner and get back to the customer by a certain time, then you had better talk to the owner and get back to the customer before that time frame ends. If you cannot reach the owner for some reason, and this sometimes can happen, then you need to call the customer back before the deadline to inform them of the delay. It might not be a pleasant conversation but it still will be better than the conversation you will have later if you never call.

People are used to people not following through today. They are accustomed to people saying what they think people want to hear just so they can get out of the situation. They don't think about later. They are only interested in taking the easy way out now. The problem with that approach is that it almost always makes things much worse for everyone.

This is just basic common sense. When you say something you create a certain level of expectation. Once that level of expectation is set it is up to you to perform at that level or better. That is why it is NEVER a good idea to commit to something you know you just cannot do just to keep people happy for the short-term.

Be honest and promise only what you know you can deliver. If you can it is always better to under promise and then over deliver. If you can make someone happy by telling them you will get back to them in 24 hours they will be thrilled when you call them back in 4 hours. But if you promise 4 hours and take 24 hours, that is not good. Always give yourself a bit of wiggle room.

Another area where responsiveness is important is the first contact or whenever someone need assistance. If a customer has to wait a long period of time before getting help, they might give up and just walk out never to return. Then you have lost a customer without ever really understanding why or even being aware that you lost that customer in the first place!

If someone leaves you a message or a voice mail or e-mail, respond to that message as quickly as you can. People love a quick response. Even if it is just a confirmation that you received their message and giving them a rough time frame for your response. This way they know that someone has their request and is working on it.

Being responsive also helps the business and employees out as well. When people are forced to wait longer than they expect, they start thinking about the situation. The longer they think about something the more they blow it out of proportion and the result is that they get angrier than they should be. All because no one responded to their message or request.

When people are left to wait and when they get angrier, two things usually happen. You spend more time trying to calm them down and getting back to their original problem. This wastes your time and the customer's time. But at the same time, the angrier a customer gets the more it is going to take to make them happy again. So the problem that might have cost you $10 to resolve quickly might now cost you $50 or $100 because you didn't respond fast enough.

Also understand that your opinion of what is appropriate as far as response time is not what matters. It is what the customer thinks is appropriate that really matters. The customer is the one who needs to be happy and satisfied not you!

5   Be Accessible

If you want to make your customers love you then you need to be as accessible as possible so your customers can find you when they need you. If you are not available when they need you they will go somewhere where they can find someone who is available!

When it comes to accessibility, there are two areas that you need to be aware of.

The first, and most commonly thought of, is when you and your business are open to your customers. If your hours are too short or restrictive, your customer may go elsewhere. They are going to do business with stores that are open when it is convenient for them to shop.

That might mean needing to be open at night or in the evenings and possibly Saturdays and Sundays as well. If you want to be popular with the most people, you need to be convenient for the most people as well.

The second type of accessibility is how accessible you are during normal business hours. Even if your business is open 24 hours a day if your customer cannot get the assistance they need when they need it, they will go elsewhere.

For example, if your business is known for long wait times, I can almost guarantee you that you are losing business just because people are not willing to even give you and your business a chance. Most people hate long waits and others just do not have the time to wait even if waiting doesn't really bother them. If you want people to buy from you, you must make it easy and quick for them.

Some businesses, such as insurance companies for example, have assigned representatives for certain customers. For example, if you have your insurance policy with a company and Bob is your agent, then you go to Bob with questions, claims and other issues. If Bob is always busy, or Bob's calls always goes to voice mail and he takes 3 days to respond, most customers will eventually look elsewhere.

If you want your customers to love you, make it easy for them to get the help or assistance they want. Make it easy for them to come in, get what they need and get out in the fastest time possible. Streamline your processes, have enough employees and salespeople around to help them so that wait times are low. If people have to wait to speak to someone or search around to find someone to help them, they are likely to leave.

Take some time to visit your competition and compare how easy it is to do business with them as compared to your business. How do you measure up?

Would people like doing business with you better or with your competition? What are your strong and weak points? Both matter because people go where there is more of what they like or less of what they don't like. You have to hit it right on both counts to make customers love you.

Create business hours that are convenient based on your customer base. Look at your competition. If they are open later or longer or on more days, consider changing your hours to make it easier for people to come to you instead of going somewhere else. Granted there may be additional costs involved in staying open longer but you might find out that those expenses are more than made up in extra business, more customers and larger sales.

Just create the best accessibility you can for your customers and chances are they will love you for it.

6 Provide Superior Value

This one is an easy one. With all things being equal, people will usually respond to the business that offers the best or superior value. Customers are people like you and I and everyone loves to get a great deal. But superior value means more than just the best price.

There are two very important parts to that first paragraph.

First of all, we said "with all things being equal" which means that there are many factors that make up what a customer considers a great or superior value. All businesses are better at some things than they are at others and sometimes you might not stack up well against your competition. So as much as you might want to believe it, all things are not equal when it comes time to figure out who has the best overall value.

The second thing is that value is much more than just price. That is why we used the term "value" instead of just saying provide the lowest price. One of the most surprising facts is that a lot of the time prices is not among the most important factors when it comes time to making a purchase!

Other factors such as quality, convenience, selection, product knowledge, value added extras and many other things all contribute to the overall value of doing business with someone. If you disagree, ask yourself a few of the following questions:

Would you knowingly purchase a poor quality product just because it costs a little less?

Would you buy from a business you did not trust to save a few dollars?

Would you drive across town to save $5?

Would you rather buy from a store that has a rewards program and provides accessories and other products free with your purchase?

Would you take time off of work to purchase something at a store that wasn't open evenings or weekends?

Would you rather go to a store that had one item of the type that you wanted or go to a store that had 20 different items but at a slightly higher price?

Would you buy from a store that delivered or would you prefer to rent a truck and pick the product up to save $20?

All of the above questions have one thing in common. They all relate to some part of the buying experience that relates to overall value.

Every one of those questions has something in it that will either increase or decrease the perceived value. Every one of those items can make the difference between a customer purchasing from you or from your competition.

So when it comes to creating the best overall value for your customers, don't stop at price. Offer value added extras and services like free delivery and other items designed to make the purchase look like a far better value in the eyes of the customers.

The great thing about approaching sales in this matter is often you can charge higher prices and still make more sales because your customer sees the overall superior value and not just the price tag.

7   Provide Superior Service

You have to just face it. People love great service. If you can provide a superior level of service than your competition, then your customers will love you. Sometimes they will even go to your business over someplace more convenient and with lower prices just because they get better or superior service from your company.

When you look at the entire customer experience, the service people receive from a business plays a huge role in the overall experience. If the service is poor, the experience will suffer. If the service is great, the experience will be made better. Even if the customer doesn't realize it, service matters to them and will affect the way they look at you and your business.

For example, let's say a customer walks into your store to buy a product. There is no one around to help him select the right product so he purchases one that he thinks will be a good choice but he lacks the knowledge to really make the right decision.

So he goes home and the product doesn't do what he needs it to do. It is too small, not powerful enough, doesn't have the right connections or fitting or whatever the problem is, it just doesn't do what the customer needed. So he returns it.

When he returns it the person taking the return understands and recommends the right product which ends up working fine and the customer has what needed in the first place. But after the initial relief wears off they realize that has there been someone there to help them in the first place, they would have saved all that time and frustration and would have bought the right product in the first place.

The result is a negative customer experience.

Another example might be having to return or exchange a purchase and having to wait on long lines or go through endless paperwork and questions in order to get a refund. Maybe you couldn't get a refund at all and had to settle for a store credit. Whatever the outcome, if you view it as excessively negative, that alone might keep you from buying there in the future. There are businesses who stress easy, no questions asked, returns for just that reason.

You goal should always be to provide the highest level of service possible for your customer. That means hiring and training knowledgeable employees and having them in sufficient numbers that people do not have to wait for a long period of time in order to get help.

If you have knowledgeable people but your customers can't get to them they might as well not be there in the first place.

Your customers should not have to seek out help or service either. It should be offered to them when they enter the store or while they are looking. In other words, successful businesses are pro-active when it comes to help and service. They don't wait to be asked, they are pro-active and offer it first.

Now when it comes to being pro-active, there is sometimes a fine line between being pro-active and harassing a customer. We should offer help to our customers but we should not keep after them or continuing to ask them as they shop. Some people are there just to look and don't plan on buying and don't want service. In those cases we should ask once and then let the customer be. We might also ask people who are on their way out if they found everything they needed or if they have any questions. This might salvage a potential lost sales because of unanswered questions.

Another area of service that is important is accurate service. All the help and assistance in the world is not going to help if you provide incorrect or incomplete information to the customer. Always remember that your customers often use the knowledge you give them to choose the right product.

If you give them wrong information, or if you don't give them all the information and leave it to them to fill in the missing parts, they might make the wrong choice. And when they realize they made the wrong choice, they will blame you.

So how do you provide superior service? Well, before you can provide superior service to anyone you have to know what kind of service your competition or other similar businesses provide their customers. Then, you take the best parts of everyone's service that they offer and you create your own superior customer service experience.

That might mean having better trained salespeople or more salespeople so access is easier.

That might mean having more checkout registers open and maybe an express register for people who have smaller purchases and want to get out faster.

That might mean holding classes on how to use your products so people have an easier and faster learning curve when it comes to using their products. This can be handy with tech products such as computers or cameras.

That might mean after an after sales support function where people can =go to get advice and questions answered.

Every little thing you can do to improve the level of service you can offer your customers will go a long way towards keeping those customers loyal to your business and also help make it easier for them to recommend you to others.

8 Provide Superior Quality

One area where some businesses fall short is their understanding in how quality affects the overall customer experience. By quality we mean just how good and reliable the products they sell, or the services they provide, are in the eyes of the customer.

The joy of a low price and the positive feelings about a great value soon vanish when the product or service we purchase fall short of our expectations. When something is not of the quality that we expect, we do not only take our frustration out on the manufacturers but also sometimes on the business who sold it to us. Though this is not necessarily fair, it is the reality that we have to deal with.

For example, for years I managed a service organization that employed field service technicians. We surveyed all our customers after we did repairs on their equipment. We noticed that we routinely received very negative surveys back on the service we performed. But when we contacted the customers, they had no problems with the service we performed. In fact, they usually were very pleased with the technician and the service.

But they failed us because they had so many problems with the product itself and they thought we were somehow responsible for the quality of the product!

As I said, it is not fair but it is our reality.

Because of this, we should be taking whatever precautions we can to make sure we sell high quality products. We should not sell inferior quality products just because they cost us less. Because the money we save on the product will be much less than the cost of that customer walking over to our competition.

The same applies to businesses that sell services. If your "product" is a service that you provide, always look to provide the best possible quality service to the customer. Don't skimp or cut corners to save a few dollars here and there. In the long run this does not save you money is COSTS you money.

Most customers place a premium on quality and reliability. Entire product brands and businesses have been built around quality and customer service. These business don't sell cheap products and they don't deliver inferior services either. In fact, they usually charge a premium price and people pay it because they understand that they are getting a quality product from a quality business.

Though you will read this again in this book, one thing we must understand that when it comes to anything related to the customer experience we cannot just give the customer what they expect to get. We must give them more than they expect in order to create a positive impression on the customer. After all, no one gets impressed if they get what they expect.

We will discuss this more in a little while but for now, let's just say that if you want your customers to really love you and your business, provide them with a selection of quality products that will do what they are supposed to do and will continue to do what they are supposed to do for a very long time. That makes customers fall in love with products and businesses.

For example, many years ago I purchased a lawn mower. I paid a pretty good price for it but it lasted many, many years. I had that mower probably twice as long as I thought I would. I was very impressed. So when it came time that it did actually stop working, there was no doubt which brand I would buy again. I bought the same brand and paid a higher price strictly on quality.

Unfortunately, the opposite holds true as well. The replacement mower I bought, from the same manufacturer, was more plastic than metal and it failed within a few years. I was not happy with that and when it came time to buy a new mower once again, I looked at every option out there and bought a different brand.

In those examples we have a very impressed customer who purchased again strictly because of high quality. He even was willing to pay a premium price. But that same customer, when faced with inferior quality, was no longer loyal and bought another brand of mower from another store.

So we can see that businesses can be made or destroyed by the quality of products they sell. It is critical to remember that when someone purchases an inferior product not only does the manufacturer suffer but the business that sold it can suffer too.

So make a commitment to become a business well known for its high quality and not just for its lower prices. Because quality issues make an impact long after a great price has been long forgotten.

9 Don't Base Everything on Price!

Now that we have discussed the impact that quality and service have on the total perceived value of a product or service, let's discuss how prices enters into things. This is important because price is often not as important as most business think it really is.

While everyone wants a great deal and no one wants to pay more than they have to for things, price is usually not the primary driving force behind whether or not to purchase or where to purchase from. In fact, most customers who are surveyed placed several things higher on their list of priorities than price!

Stop and think about this for a moment:

If you tried to think of the best products and businesses in your neighborhood or area, which are the ones that immediately pop into your head? It is usually the products that are the most respected and the businesses where you get the best experience. That is because your mind usually goes to perceived quality and customer experience rather than price.

Now switch gears a bit and think about which businesses or products have the lowest prices. Chances are you would come up with a whole different set of businesses and products. That is because high quality and low prices are usually not thought about at the same time.

For example, if you were in the mood to purchase a car, you would have a choice between a standard vehicle, a low priced economy vehicle or a luxury vehicle. Now all of these cars would get you from point A to point B. But some manufacturers place an emphasis on quality and luxury instead of price. In fact, their prices are often 10's of thousands higher for their cars and they sell A TON of them to people who value quality over price.

The exception to this rule might be when customers are looking for a brand name product that is available at several places in their area or on-line. If they can get the exact same product for a lower price, then price might matter. After all they are purchasing the exact same product so quality is not the issue. In these cases, prices does matter and you have to be competitive.

For example, if you want to buy a Ford car and one dealer wants $25,000 for that car while another dealer wants $23,500, then you might want to buy from the dealer with the lower price and pocket the $1,500 difference.

After all the car is the same regardless of where you bought it. So in this case, price does matter.

But it still doesn't mean you have to be the lowest price. There are so many other things that for some customers are even more important than price for their particular reasons.

In the car example above, if the higher priced dealer offers evening service hours, priority service appointments for buyers, free loaner cars, free oil changes and other perks for customers who purchase their cars from that dealership, it might sway people into paying the premium and buying the car from them even though the price is higher! It doesn't matter what it costs you to provide these "extras" to the customer. What matters is the value the customer places on these extras.

As we have already said, entire businesses have thrived on being built on overall value and service rather than price. Businesses built on price are not always a customer's first choice. In fact, there is a market segment of customers who like low priced businesses and a whole other market segment for customers who want quality and convenience over everything else.

Much of where your business lies is going to depend on the industry or market your business is positioned in. If you are selling high-end products or expensive items, then stressing quality is almost always the best place to focus you efforts.

Generally speaking, the more expensive your products are the more focus should be placed on quality and support and less on price. Don't ignore price as it should always be a consideration but don't let that be your prime driver.

But if you deal in everyday products or necessities that customers have to buy then price becomes more important. Items like toilet paper, cleaning supplies, home supplies, clothes and other similar items that we need to buy constantly become more price oriented. But even then, we should not abandon the quality aspect all together.

The best and most successful business are the ones that combine price and quality to create an overall value and level of experience that is far better than the competition. You can do that as long as you concentrate on the total customer experience instead of just one small part of it.

10   Provide Excellent
After Sale Support

Here is one area where more businesses and employee miss the boat than any other part of the customer experience. They are under the impression that as long as everything from the initial contact to the actual purchase goes extremely well then they are finished. That is not only untrue it is a very dangerous attitude for a business to have these days.

If you truly want customers to love you and rave about your business, you should create a culture where the actual purchase is only the beginning. In other words, you should create an after sale support system that addresses customer needs well after they get their purchase home and start using it.

Think about the time when you purchased something and got it home and it either didn't work or you had questions about something. You call the place where you bought it from and they tell you they don't take the product back but you have to call the manufacturer for service. Or, you call to ask a question and there is no way to get an answer to that question.

Either you can't find someone to talk to or when you can actually talk to someone they don't have the training or knowledge to give you the right answer.

After sales support and service are extremely important when it comes to certain products. If you bought a head of lettuce from the supermarket, you might not have many questions about that lettuce. But if you bought a brand new home entertainment center and cannot program the remote, you would have questions. When you have question, you want the place where you bought it give you the answers.

Just try to go into a big box or discount store with your questions and see how far it gets you. Unless they specialize in one type of product, you are not likely to find skilled people to answer your questions. Those types of stores are so focused on sales volume and low prices that they pay their employees fairly low wages so the turnover is high and the knowledge level low.

That is an area where you can capture market share by providing highly trained people to resolve problems, answer questions and take care of the customer's needs after the sale is completed. Depending on the product lines you offer this could help you capture a larger market share, more customers and more sales.

Plus it will help you take your current customers and turn them into ambassadors for your business all by offering a premium level of after sales support!

Another area that falls under the umbrella of after sales support are the refund or exchange processes. If they are too restrictive, time consuming or difficult, this will probably turn customers off and send them elsewhere for their next purchase. This is a common reason for losing customers.

Now we understand that having these policies in place is important for the health and well-being of the business. After all we cannot have people bringing back defective products years after their purchase and demanding refunds or bringing back product bought elsewhere for refunds at your store. You need procedures and you should have them. But those procedures need to be fair both to the business and the customers.

One common complaint is that it was so easy to purchase the product but then so difficult to return it. This gives the customer the feeling that all you are interested in is taking their money and don't really care about resolving their problems or giving that money back. You can avoid this by streamlining the return or exchange policy and making it less difficult or time consuming. Most customers will really appreciate that.

You can accomplish this by having more employees dedicated to processing returns or exchanging products. It is amusing to see some businesses that have 18 cashiers waiting to take the customer's money while they have just one person handling returns and exchanges along with 127 other job duties and responsibilities. One indication of not having enough coverage is seeing long lines constantly at the refund desk. If you see that, you have a problem.

Another common complaint concerns the time frame after purchase in which products can be returned or exchanged. Some businesses are very restrictive and have a very short window in which customers can return or exchange their purchases. This can frustrate customers especially when that window of opportunity does not really give them adequate time to fully check out or evaluate their purchase. If you want to make customers really happy, give them a longer window to return or exchange. This sends the right message to your customers.

Another area of after sale support which has a high perceived value is a repair service when it comes to high ticket items which are usually repaired instead of replaced.

If you can offer a service department to handle service problems that makes it easier for your customers to have their issues taken care of without dealing with the manufacturer or even boxing up their equipment and mailing it off to the manufacturer.

After sales service is something that can be very attractive to both the customer and the business itself. It is also a nice money make at times. You can offer your customers the security and peace of mind that comes with a service contract while creating another revenue stream for your business.

Over the years I have been involved in many businesses both as an employee and as a consultant and in almost every single one they focused on sales and treated support functions as an afterthought unless they brought money into the business. The almost universal feeling was that once you had the customer's money you concentrated on the next sale and forgot about the customer and the sale you just made. Naturally this is a dangerous philosophy.

I also have noticed that in the past businesses who focused solely on sales and ignored or treated after sale support had a far greater chance of going out of business. While you cannot make a generalized statement about why unrelated businesses failed, I am confident that their attitudes towards their customers played a significant role in the failure of their business. You cannot treat customers poorly and expect them to keep coming back.

Very often when people decide which product they want to purchase the question of after sales support becomes a very highly motivating factor in deciding where to purchase. Most of the time the dealer who sells and repairs will capture a much higher market share than the dealer who sells it and then tells the customer to go somewhere else to get their problems resolved.

Now you have to decide which type of dealer you want to be in your neighborhood.

11 Be Honest & Truthful

This is one of the easiest ones to explain. Businesses that are honest and trustworthy in the eyes of the customer are the one who stand the test of time. It is the business that deceives or openly lies to its customers that finds itself with the going out of business sign in the front window.

It is unfortunate that there are so many businesses out there today that exist solely to make sales at any cost whether they provide good service and good products to their customers or not. There is far too much of this going on today and there are more and more customers who are starting to get fed up and refuse to deal with that sort of behavior any more.

We have all experienced some kind of consumer fraud or other activity at some point in our lives. It happens far more often that it should be and the really sad part of it is that it sometimes never makes it into the papers or news until it gets to the point where many people were cheated or taken advantage of.

We all know how it works. Deceptive advertising, misleading sales, bait and switch, false scarcity and every other known trick in the book. All designed to get you and your money.

We also have businesses that technically follow the letter of the law but push the boundaries to the breaking point. In other words, they don't actually break the law but they come as close to doing so as they possibly can.

I had a friend who worked for a tire company. People would call up to see if they had particular tire in stock. His manager told him to always say yes when someone asked him if something was in stock. The idea was once someone actually walked in to purchase that tire they would be told they just sold the last set but they had similar tires at a slightly higher price. They were banking on the fact that most customers would just say OK because they had already invested time in coming to the shop.

They also bank on the customer thinking this was just an unfortunate coincidence. After all, things do happen like that. But the problem is over time they will hear friends and co-workers tell of the same experience and they will realize how that n=business really works. The result is the next time you needed tires or whatever that business sold you would look elsewhere.

The amusing part of this is that people usually really appreciate it when a business is honest with them. They appreciate being told over the phone that something is out of stock. They don't want to waste time. It is more than being honest it is being respectful of the customer and their time.

The same holds true for honest and truthful information regarding the products that you sell. Do not try and sell someone something just because you get a higher commission or the price is higher. If a lower priced model will better suit the customer's needs, then suggest that model. Your customer will be impressed that you didn't try to upsell them something they didn't need in order to make a few dollars more.

An extension of that would also be telling people that your product will do things it won't really do because you want to lose the sale. When you do this you not only waste the customer's time, you also open yourself up to more refunds and exchanges which just wastes everyone's time.

If you advertise a product, have enough of that product in stock to fulfill the anticipated demand. If you run out offer a rain check at the same price. Do NOT advertise a really great price on something and then tell them you are out of it when they come in and try and sell them something more expensive. Not only is this technically illegal, it creates a lot of anger and frustration on the part of the customer.

So if you want your customers to love you and be happy with you and your business, make sure your business is as honest and trustworthy as possible. If there is ever a gray area, make your decision on what is best for the customer. This might cost you a few more pennies now but result in a lot more sales in the future.

12 Follow Through on What You Say You Will Do

As we have already stated, customers are people just like you and I and we all expect people to do what they say they are going to do. This means keeping their promises and following up on what they have committed to doing.

Unfortunately there are many businesses and people who fail to do what they committed to and this creates problems for the rest of us. It is perfectly normal these days for customers to be suspicious of everyone and to not believe what they are being told. This is the customer's way of protecting themselves against being cheated or taken advantage of.

Because of this, your customers will initially be wary or suspicious of you and your business as well. Only after you have demonstrated several times that you can be trusted and that you mean what you say will they begin to let their guard down and trust you. That breakthrough is very important when it comes to creating lifelong customers.

But like we said, there are businesses who don't follow that path with their customers. Here are some of the approaches some business and their employees use that create negative customer experiences:

One tactic many people and businesses use when dealing with angry customers is to promise them whatever it is that they want to hear just to get out of that situation. But the problem with that approach is that eventually someone is going to have to get back to that customer and tell them the truth. At that point the customer's expectations will have risen to an even higher level and things will really get ugly!

Other businesses will make commitments and may even make efforts to fulfill those commitments but they do not keep the customer informed throughout the process. Sometimes the process involved is something that takes time and many steps in order to complete. Other times several people are involved and we must wait for one person to accomplish their part before we can proceed. In these cases we need to keep the customer informed throughout the process.

Many times we tell the customer that we will call them back by a certain date or time. We chose that date or time because we felt that everything should be completed by that time.

But as we said in the previous paragraph, sometimes we have limited or no control over part of the process and things take longer than we originally thought.

When this happens, we should still be calling back the customer if only to let them know we are still working on things are giving them a status update. We need to do this for two important reasons.

First, we made a commitment to the customer and we need to always stand by our commitments. If you said you would call back or do something by a certain time, then you must make that call or complete the task. Even if it is just a call to let them know you are still working on things and then give them a new date, that is what you need to do. Remember it is YOOUR credibility on the line here because it was you who made that commitment.

The other reason for keeping the customer informed is that you and your business are the ones who have the direct relationship with the customer. You either sold the product or made a commitment to them. By keeping them informed, you can let them know you are doing your best but that someone outside your company is the reason for the hold up or delay. While this might not make the customer happy, they will still know that you are doing your best but that someone else is causing the problem. This might not restore your relationship with the customer completely but you will have at least informed them of the reasons for the delay.

There will be times when you make a good faith commitment and have all the intentions of keeping that commitment to the customer. But something goes wrong or you forget about something until it's too late. In those cases you need to contact the customer and take responsibility for the error. Apologize to them and don't make excuses. Just ask for their understanding and patience and then go into overdrive to resolve the issue and fulfill that commitment.

Which all brings about a concept that might seem a little strange but happens to work very well.

That concept is:

13 Under Promise then Over Deliver

Whenever we make a promise or tell a customer something, we set a certain level of expectation. Once a level of expectation is set, then it is up to us to reach that level or exceed it. Anything less than achieving that level of expectation will result in an angry and disappointed customer.

So it makes sense to set that level of expectation as low as possible. But unfortunately, we cannot set it too low or our customers will be unhappy because their own expectations were higher than that and they might just go elsewhere instead of giving us the chance to help them out.

So setting expectations is kind of a balancing act where you want to set their expectations higher than what they thought they were going to get but lower than what you really believe you are capable of providing. This way the customers are pleased and you have given yourself a bit of a cushion when it comes time to deliver on your commitment.

For example, if a customer has to order a part for one their products and you think you could have that part in 10 days, then you might tell them it would arrive in 15 days. If this made the customer happy then you would leave it at that and call them when it came in. If they expressed displeasure you could tell them you would try to expedite it and get it in 12 days or 11 days but you should never tell them you can get it in 5 days when it you know it will take 10 just to make them happy.

No one really complains when they receive something better or faster than what they were told. If you told them 15 days and it arrived in 6 days, they would be thrilled. But if you told them it would arrive in 6 days but it took 10, they would be disappointed or even upset. In other words, give yourself some "wiggle room" to make as sure as you can be that you will be able to deliver on your promise or commitment.

This is important because sometimes customers make other plans or commitments based on what you told them. Using the example above, maybe they arranged for other work to be done on their equipment that required that part. So if you told them 6 days and they scheduled the work to be done 6 days later and the part didn't arrive in time that would cause problems for the customer.

This doesn't mean that we shouldn't always try to do or give the best to our customer. We should always try to provide the very best level of service possible to every customer. But we need to do that in a responsible fashion. We should never make commitments we know we can't keep just to make someone happy or close a sale.

Remember that "stuff happens" and that we must take those things into consideration when making promises or commitments. Our customers don't care about our problems or why we couldn't do something that we committed to doing for them. All they know is that you made a commitment and failed to follow through on it.

So let's try to do two things from this point forward.

The first is to never over promised and then under deliver. Always give yourself a little cushion and make our commitments and promises to our customers more easily achievable. We can surprise our customers with something better or faster but we must never disappoint them by missing a deadline or failing to fulfill our commitment.

The second thing we must do from this point forward is to keep our customers informed every step of the way so they know what is going on and that they know we are trying our best to make things happen. This will help our customers understand the value of doing business with you and your company.

Our promises and commitments are at the heart of our relationships with our customers. We need them to trust in us and believe in us. Once we achieve that we have created customers who love us and will continue to do business with us. Trust will take us a long way in creating powerful and long lasting relationships with our customers.

14   Respond Quickly
– Within 24 Hours

This tip will not only help the customer but will also help make your life easier and more productive as well. That is because the faster you respond to a customer problem, issue or phone call, the easier it will be for everything that follows.

How quickly you respond tells the customer several things about you and your business. A fast response tells them that you feel your customers are important. A slow response tells them that you do not feel your customers are that important or that there are other things you feel are more important to spend your time on.

How quickly you respond also tells the customer what type of customer culture your business has. A wait or rapid response tells your customer that your business is customer focused and that the overall customer experience is something that is important to them.

A slow response, or having to wait on long lines or spending long amounts of time on hold signifies that the customer is not held as much of a priority and that resources are dedicated elsewhere in the business.

So we can immediately see how the amount of waiting or response time can create a certain perception in the minds of the customers. It makes little difference whether or not that perception is accurate or not. That is because how your customer perceives things to be IS their reality! So if they think you don't care about your customers because you took 4 days to respond to a message that is all that matters to them.

Another important reason to respond quickly is because the human brain tends to distort the reality of things as time goes on. The longer you take to respond means the longer the customer has to think about things, get madder or more frustrated and blow things all out of proportion. So what might have been a simple or minor problem could transform itself into a complete nightmare once you do talk to the customer.

Studies have shown a direct correlation between response time and customer satisfaction. Businesses who respond faster are almost always rated higher in terms of customer satisfaction. It is a little thing that can carry huge benefits for you and your business.

Now the question should be "How fast should I be?"

There is no fixed or standard answer. So I will give you the two most common answers to that question. You need to be as fast as you can and you have to be as fast as your customer expects you to be. If you can hit both those objectives then you should be in great shape as far as response time is concerned.

It is always good to create a business model with processes in place that focuses on customer response time and addressing customer needs and inquiries. That means making it not only easier for the customers to contact you but also for you to contact the customer. That means having multiple ways for customers to get in touch with you and for you to get in touch with them.

E-mail is a great way for most inquiries because people on both ends can access their e-mail whenever they have a minute or two of spare time. While a telephone call must be answered the exact minute someone calls you, e-mails can be answered as they arrive or minutes or hours afterwards. There is no "phone tag", leaving messages, or coordinating of schedule so you can find a time when both of you are available to talk.

I like e-mail because it allows me to process 3-4 times more customer inquiries and complaints in the same amount of time. It is much more efficient and easier for me to handle e-mails and forward them to others as well.

So when a customer has an issue that someone else needs to handle, I can simply forward that e-mail to the right person, copy in the customer and they can take it from there. This can also be accomplished in seconds rather than the 15 minutes it might have taken to call the customer or the other person back and explain things.

I also like e-mail because I can set a level of expectation in the e-mail that becomes a permanent record for the customer. Sometimes we might say one thing but over a few hours the customer remembers something else. For example, I might say I will get back to you later today or possibly tomorrow but all the customer hears is "today". If they have the e-mail they will be reminded of what I really said. Of course, if you just said "I'll have an answer tomorrow" and not mentioned the possibility of today you would be better off!

E-mail also allows us to sometimes use something called an "auto responder" which allows the e-mail server to automatically send out a reply e-mail confirming that we received the e-mail. You can place any message you want in the return e-mail including any time you might be out of the store or office such as vacation time or holiday closures.

Doing this will make people aware of when you are out so they won't think you were just ignoring them.

E-mail also allows you to forward messages to others while you are away as well.

But all things considered, if you promise or commit to a 24 hour or same day reply to all e-mails that should be sufficient for most industries and situations. Of course, if you are involved in critical products or services such as medical products and services, you might require a faster or more immediate response. Whatever is considered the norm for your industry or market segment should be your MINIMUM response time. As usual faster is better.

For those using the telephone and dealing with phone messages, same day response is almost a requirement rather than a desired time frame. If messages are left at night or later on in the day then a return phone call the next morning should be the objective. You must understand that somewhere in the mind of the customer they assume you will get their message within minutes or within the hour. It makes no difference if you are out sick or on vacation in the mind of the customer. Unless you make some kind of response, or have someone make it for you, the customers will become upset if they do not get a response within what they feel is a reasonable amount of time.

If you want your customers to be impressed with you and your business, then give them a response time that is faster than what they expect.

In other words, exceed their expectations and you will create an impression in their minds that they really matter to your business. All it takes is a little more effort and the mindset to respond faster and you will soon have a truckload of customers who love you and your business!

15 Think Home Runs Not Singles

Most people go into business with the idea of providing quality products or service to their customers and being able to grow the business over time. No one goes into business with the idea of failing and losing their money. After all, to open up a business takes time and money and people go through all of that to get rich and build their business.

But the problem with many businesses, business owners and employees is that they don't take that vision or idea far enough. They want to provide quality services and sell quality products but only up to a point. In other words, they want to be good enough to succeed but not much above that.

The problem with that idea or philosophy is that with all the competition around for most businesses today you simply cannot be "good enough" and expect to succeed. Stated very simply, good enough usually is not good enough these days. So we need to change our attitude and change our philosophy.

Though I hate sports metaphors, this one really hits the nail on the head so I am going to use it anyway.

If I am a baseball player looking to break into the big leagues, I need to perform at a certain level or beyond or I will never get a chance because the competition is so very high at that level. If I go up to the plate every time just looking to make contact and hit a single I am not likely to get very far at all and might never get close to the big leagues. I might hit well but singles hitters are not the players who get noticed unless there are other things in play.

But if I go up to the plate looking and thinking home run, then I am going to swing harder, concentrate better and push myself to make better contact and increase my power. After all, it's easier to hit singles than it is to hit home runs. That is why home run hitters are more in demand, get noticed more and get paid a lot more.

When it comes to your business, are you a singles hitter? Are you the business that looks to see what their customers want and then provides that but doesn't look for more ways to help the customer?

Or are you the business who wants to hit a home run for every customer. If a customer comes in and wants something, are you the one who gives that to them but also offers them more? Are you the business that is satisfied with just meeting expectations but knocking those expectations out of the park?

Let me give you the unvarnished truth right here and now.

The world is full of businesses who are singles hitters. Business of all types and sizes are full of employees who are singles hitter as well. These employees and business are those places where people go for an average experience that is not usually memorable for them. They rarely walk out with any kind of "wow factor" or positive impression. Is that what you want for your customers? Do you want them to think of your business as the place to go "for an average experience"?

I don't think so. Because if you are that type of business, I want to be your competitor. Because businesses who look to take the most and give back the least are the easiest businesses to steal customers from!

Why?

Because when you don't swing to hit home runs, you never push yourself to get better. So others look at you and your business and see so many ways to offer their customers more than they get with you. They will capitalize on your weaknesses and steal your customers away. Chances are you will never be aware of this until it might be too late.

If you want your customers to love you, you have to give them a reason. You have to earn their love. You have to earn that love by doing your very best to provide your customers with the best overall customer experience possible.

You can do it if you are willing to make the effort and perhaps spend a few extra dollars. But this is not about money or a little extra effort. It is all about giving your customers the type of experience that will make them talk about your business with friends and family members.

So the next time a customer walks through your doors, are going to step up and try to hit a home run or are you going to just hit a single. I'm hoping you swing for the fences because if you don't you can bet your life that your competition will.

16 Listen to Your Customers

Our customers tell us things every single day but sometimes we just either aren't aware of what they are telling us or we just don't really care. Either way, whenever we don't listen to what the customer is telling us we place our business at risk and increase the possibility of creating negative customer experiences.

Most of the time we listen to customers is when they have problems or are speaking to us about something. They are either telling us what they like or dislike about us and our business. Sometimes they might make comments about our competition and the differences between us and them. This is the most obvious form of communication between the business and the customer.

But customers also communicate with us in other ways as well. These are less obvious ways that we either ignore or aren't even aware of in the first place. But through these other methods of communication we can usually learn a lot more about how our customers feel about our business.

Do you really look at your customers and try to evaluate their thoughts and moods? Do you stop and try and look at their facial expressions and body language? Do they look happy or sad, calm or frustrated? Sometimes people will not stop and talk to you about things but you can easily see it in their faces. But only if you take the time to look and really see.

For example, if you look at your customers while they are waiting on a long line to pay for their purchase, you might see really frustrated and angry faces on that line. So that would give you the realization that your lines are too long and that this might be angering your customers. After all, if this is more the norm than the occasional issue, your customer might start going somewhere else.

The strange thing is that many customers might be angry or upset and never voice those feelings to you. It will be very clear from their body language and facial expressions but they might feel afraid or intimidated to tell you in person. Some might write a letter once they get home but most will just walk out never to return. By that time it is too late. You need to be pro-active instead of reactive.

It is also a great idea to make it easy for your customers to tell you how they feel. The easier you make it for them to express themselves, the more information you will get about your business.

There are several ways you can accomplish this.

You can have the old fashion suggestion box where customers can fill out a card with comments and suggestions. This removes the potential intimidation of speaking to someone face to face about anything negative.

You can use a survey company to survey your customers if you get their personal information when they purchase. Surveys can be done over the phone, online, or through the mail. Generally speaking go with whatever method is the easiest for your customers. They are far more apt to respond when you make it easier for them to do so.

You could use an employee stationed at the exits to do an informal exit survey by just asking them if they found everything they needed and if everything went well with their visit. Just the asking of the question might open the door and remove some of the hesitation for the customers. But some customers will still not say anything in person because they feel awkward or afraid.

The key is to be aware and be observant. We are usually observant when it comes to the sales process when we look for people that need help. In that example we look for someone who looks puzzled or confused and we respond to those clues and offer assistance. We need to follow that same process when it comes to all aspects of our business.

Customers provide us with many forms of communication when it comes to how they feel about their business. We need to take advantage of all those forms and develop our employees so that they know what to look for and how to notice certain things.

Smiles are good. We don't want to see frowns.

Happy is good. We don't want to see anger or frustration.

Relaxed people are good. Aggressive people, not so much.

Then there are the obvious things that we don't really have to look very hard for but still might be important. People that are yelling or demanding more help or more open checkouts. People who leave full carts and walk out of the store. People who are very aggressive and confrontational. All of these are examples of people who are not happy with your business.

Now there will be times when people are angry for no real or appropriate reason. In other words, people sometimes come in looking for trouble or have expectations that are unreasonable or downright off the wall. When we run into those situations, or when people make complaints that are unrealistic, we need to keep those in the proper perspective.

For example, if you receive a complaint about long wait times because a customer had to wait 3 minutes and they were in a hurry, that is not a valid complaint and should not require a change in procedure, manpower or processes. If the wait was 10 or 20 minutes that might be different. But certainly not 2 or 3 minutes.

So we need to understand how our customers feel about us and that requires not only listening to the words they speak but also their body language and their facial expressions. We need to sometimes solicit information from our customers even though we might not necessarily want to hear what their responses might be.

But then we need to objectively process that information and use it properly. Some responses may be realistic while others will be totally off the wall. We need to not only gather as much information as possible but also use it responsively once we have it.

Listening to our customers enable us to be pro-active and address problems and situations faster and before they become major problems. This results in a better customer experience for every customer and fewer problems in the future for those same customers. No business is perfect but the ones who are pro-active and take care of issues and problems when they are small and when they first occur will be the ones their customers will love.

17   Never Assume

I never really understood why we need the word "assume" in our vocabulary. A far better word, which usually is more accurate, is the word "guess". Because whenever we assume something, we are really guessing. And when it comes to customer service and the overall customer experience, it is never a good idea to guess. We should know.

There is an old saying that goes "when you assume you make an "as out of u and me". That is because unless we have a certain amount of information, there is no way we can make the best and most informed decisions. When information is missing and we are left to "connect the dots" the potential for making errors or mistakes gets much greater.

That is why asking questions and gathering information is critical when it comes to customer service. We just finished discussing how to listen to our customers and that is an important part of the process.

But we also have to understand the importance of asking the right questions so that we can do the right thing and make the right responses.

Think of the information gathering process between you and the customer as a large funnel. The large part at the top are all the potential problems, issues and resolutions at the start of the process. At this point you have very little idea of what the problem really is and what you should do to resolve it. If the customer doesn't know which product they need, you don't have much information to narrow down the selection. If the customer has a problem, you don't know much about that as well.

But as you ask questions to get more information you eliminate certain things and you move further down to the narrower part of the funnel. You eliminate or qualify certain product selections or you get closer to understanding the problem. The more questions you ask, the more information you get and the few options remain available to you. In the process you get closer and closer to the bottom of the funnel.

Eventually you get all the information that is available and it is up to you to either recommend the right product, provide the best overall resolution or determine the proper course of action. When we make decisions in this manner those decisions are called "informed decisions".

They are informed decisions because we made them based on real information and not on assumptions or guesswork.

This is important because, as surprising as this might seem, sometimes the customers don't even know what they want. They might think they know but they might not have all the information or have the understanding to make the right decisions. That is what salesmen are there for when it comes to deciding which is the right product for the application. Hopefully the salesman has the background and knowledge to better match the right product with the need.

Asking questions require specific knowledge to not only understand the answers but to know which questions to ask. Every question should be designed to either confirm that something is right or to eliminate something from the process.

For example, if your customer is looking to buy a washing machine you might ask them how many people are in the household or how often they do wash. If they do wash just once a week then that should eliminate the really large capacity and more expensive machines. But if they do 15 loads of wash a week because there are 7 people in the household then that would eliminate the smaller machines and make you concentrate on the bigger models.

Another example might be when it comes to resolving a problem. Before you can come up with the right resolution, you need to understand exactly what the problem is. This is important because sometimes even the customer doesn't understand what the real problem is. They might think it is one thing when in fact the real problem is something else.

For example, a customer might come in and be angry because the new product they bought is defective because it doesn't work properly. Now you could just take it back and give them another one but that might not resolve the problem. Instead, you should ask questions designed to provide exactly what happened and what was done that lead up to the problem.

You might discover that there is nothing wrong with the product at all. It might have been caused by the customer because they were not aware of how they are supposed to operate the product. When that is the case all you need to do is explain the right way, possibly demonstrate it for them, and then the problem would be solved without having to do an exchange at all.

Sometimes we have what we think is a common problem because this has happened so many times in the past. So we just assume this is the same thing and fast forward to the generic resolution that has worked so well for us in the past. Now this might work or it might not if the problem was really something different.

If you want to have the greatest chance at success with every customer in every possible situation, then take the time to ask the right questions and narrow down what the real problem or situation really is. Only then can you provide accurate information, make the best possible choices and make those important informed decisions.

When you are able to do this you wind up resolving situations more accurately, you make the best suggestions and recommendations and you waste far less of both the customer's time and your time as well. When this happens everyone is happier and more satisfied.

Sometimes you have to do this in a somewhat careful or tactful nature because the customer might have already made their own assumptions and jumped to their own conclusions. Using the same example as above, they may have already convinced themselves that the product is defective and may resist your attempts to get to the bottom of the problem.

When this happens you need to reassure the customer that you have their best interests at heart and truly want to help them resolve their problem. Sometimes that will help calm things down and get the customer to answer your questions. But sometimes even then they will resist and insist on a particular resolution.

When this happens, and you give in to the customer's request, then you run the risk of prolonging the problem. If the customer was the cause of the original problem and you do not educate the customer, they will continue to do the same thing and the problem will continue and possibly escalate.

That is why we should use every skill and technique possible to get the opportunity to ask the right questions and get the right answers. Because once you are able to accomplish this, you have a much better success rate with the customer.

There is one more thing we want to discuss when it comes to asking questions and making decisions. There usually will come a time when you have asked all the right questions and received all the information you can possibly get. But even then you will still have several options or possibilities. When this occurs you will have to use your best judgment and pick what you feel is the best possible option.

When we insist on getting more information to narrow things down to the perfect single solution we sometimes get what is often referred to as "paralysis by analysis" which means we never make a decision because we are always looking for more information.

Usually if we can get to the 90% certainty point we are in good shape to make the decision. At this point we should process all the reaming options and make what we feel is the best decision.

When this happens consider letting the customer become part of the decision making process. Customers are generally more willing to accept a resolution when they are part of the process.

But whatever you do, ask the right questions, listen to the answers and you will make more customers happy in less time with fewer mistakes.

18 Create Relationships with Customers

Customers are like any other human being in that they like to feel appreciated and valued by the people and things around. When it comes to the businesses they purchase through, they want to feel that they are more than just a customer. They want to feel wanted.

Your customers will be more loyal and will keep doing business with you if they feel they are appreciated and are a valued part of your business. They like to feel as though their patronage is important to the business and that the business cares about them.

While the type and size of your business will often determine the type or depth of the relationship you form with your customers, there are a few things every business of any size can do to make their customers feel special and appreciated. All your employees should be instructed on these behaviors so that they can deliver the right message to your customer.

Say Hello

Some people underestimate the value of a sincere greeting. A nice greeting sets the tone for everything that follows. It makes the customer feel good and also at times can start a conversation that helps us determine the customer's needs for that visit. The greeting is also the start of the customer experience and a positive start is always a good thing.

Having someone at the door helps both in greeting the customer and also asking them if they need any help. This kind of pro-active gestured is universally well received by all customers. It shows you care that they get what they need and are willing to help them get what they want or resolve their problems.

Say Thank You

Manners have seemed to go by the wayside these days with volume becoming more important than relationships or caring about other people. We have often replaced "Thank You!" with "Next!" when it comes to dealing with customers.

Whatever the reason for the customer's visit, make sure someone says thank you at least once during the visit. If a salesman is involved he or she should say thank you before sending the customer to the cashier. The cashier should always say "Thank you and have a nice day" after processing the customer's order.

This is not a business practice. It is just good manners and something we should all do whether we are in a business setting or not.

Say Goodbye

If your business is a retail establishment where customers routinely come and go such as a big box store or a supermarket or grocery store, have someone at the exit to say thank you and goodbye to the customers as they leave. You can also ask if they found everything they needed and perhaps salvage a lost sale or two. But just saying goodbye is a nice and positive way to end the customer experience.

Remember and Use their Names

If your business is on the smaller side, or if your business assigns specific customers to specific people all the time, it is a really great idea to make an effort to remember people's names. There is nothing more personal and makes someone feel appreciated than someone remembering their name.

For example, "Good morning, how can I help you?" is a nice greeting but "Good morning, Bob, how can I help you?" is much more powerful and personal because you used the customer's actual name in the greeting. You personalized it and have shown the customer that they are important enough for you to make the effort to remember their name.

This is a small gesture that carries a big reward in the eyes of the customer. If your business is the type that deals with repeat customers and is small enough so that you can remember their names, make every effort to do so and they will love you for it. It makes them feel like "part of the family".

Get Slightly Personal with Them!

A little bit of human touch when dealing with customers also goes a long way. Instead of sticking 100% on business, try injecting a bit of slightly person conversation into the conversation. It might be something generic like the weather and what they are doing this weekend to something specific that you might know about them. This adds a personal touch to the customer experience that makes people relax, feel welcome and feel valued.

When doing this, however, take care not to get too personal. There must be boundaries between you and the customer so the conversation should not get too personal unless you already have that kind of relationship with the customer. If there is any doubt, stay on the slightly less personal side. Remember the intent is to make the customer relax and feel good not make them feel awkward or uncomfortable.

Personalized Communications

We all get bombarded with all kinds of "junk" mail or spam e-mails. While advertising and promotion are necessary parts of all business growth, we can take steps to make them more customer friendly.

One effective method of making correspondence more personal is to use the customer's name in the mailing or e-mail. Sending out a bulk e-mail or print ad to 5,000 people is not personal. But if we can have their name in the heading or throughout the text that will not only make the customer feel better but usually increases response as well. You can use a word processor for changing print ads or a mailing list program that auto inserts names for e-mails.

Another technique that is not only more personal but also converts higher is to use selective mailings where people only get offers and advertisements based on products they already have purchased. So the senior citizen customer does not get ads for the latest skateboards and the teenager does not get ads for denture adhesive. Add that to including their name and this will make the customer feel more important, get them to read the actual ad or e-mail and convert higher as well.

Special discounts or Offers

Nothing says you are appreciated than a little bit more money in your pocket from customer appreciation special deals or offers.

Showing your customers that you care about them by giving them special sales or discounts is one great way of showing your appreciation. This helps you establish a relationship with each other.

You can notify special customers of these events and discounts with letters, or even better, a personal phone call letting them know of the event. This can be extremely useful if you know someone is in the market for a particular product and you know it is going on sale soon. A little call to make them aware of this will not only help you generate more sales but will make your customer feel more valued and appreciated.

Keep in mind any time you show your customer that you were thinking about them, or any time your customer realizes that you did something for their benefit or that you took the time to remember their name and use it, you will help create deeper and more mutually beneficial relationship.

Today competition is so strong and so pervasive, sometimes creating strong relationships with existing customers might mean the difference between the overall success and failure of the business. Take the time and make the effort to create relationships with your customer and they will love you for it.

19   Be the Hero for Your Customer

Here is one way we can take any customer and help turn that customer into a customer for life. In many cases all it takes is taking one additional step or be willing to go the extra mile for the customer.

This is an easy one. It really is. There are so many people out there today who are not willing to take one more step or do one more thing either because they don't have to, because it isn't in their job description or because they won't be getting anything out of their effort. This kind of attitude is all over these days and some customers have become accustomed to it.

But just because they have become accustomed to it doesn't mean they like it. It doesn't mean they don't want someone to help them or for someone to show some initiative in a certain situation. This kind of attitude is important when it comes to showing customer just how important they are to you and your business.

We have all been in situation where people have just refused to help us once the situation gets to a certain point.

You know the employee we are talking about. The one that writes down a phone number for someone to call and gives it to us instead of making the call himself. Or the employer that could call the manufacturer and intercede on our behalf but refuses to do so.

If you want to make your customers love you, show them some love and support in return. Go the extra mile, take the extra step, do more than you are supposed to do. This is not a responsibility, it is a culture that you create within your business. You don't tell employees how to treat customers you SHOW them. You lead by example by providing more than you need to and more than your competition does.

Your customers deserve to be helped. They are doing business with your company and giving your company their hard earned money. They have placed their faith in your business and you need to show them that their faith has not been misplaced. There are too many businesses in this world that refuse to do more than they have to for their customers.

Don't let your business join that group.

20 Make it Awfully Difficult for Them to Leave!

When a customer is doing business with your business, it is because they are either getting to know your business or already have established a certain comfort level with your business. Because of this, you will have a certain advantage over your competition in your area. You will likely have that advantage as long as you remain dedicated to keep it.

Customers are people and people are creatures of habit. If they like something, or if they feel comfortable with something, they will continue to use it until they have a reason to go somewhere or try somewhere else. If you want your business to succeed and have loyal customers, you must try to never give any customer a reason to look or go elsewhere.

Think about that for a minute. Think about the times in your life when you had things you liked or were comfortable with and you kept using them even though there might have been other, and possibly better alternatives out there for you. Chances are you could easily come up with several examples in just your life alone.

Two things happen when you give a customer a reason to look elsewhere. They will either find a better or more convenient alternative or they will realize that your business is not all that special. Even if the alternative they come across is exactly the same as your business in terms of product, selection and pricing that business will often appear better because they had not given you a negative experience recently. Either way, your business might stand to lose a customer and all the business that customer represents solely because you gave them a reason to look elsewhere.

What good businesses do is to try their best not to provide any customer with any reason to leave or even look elsewhere. Once you do that, you dramatically increase the chances that customers will leave you for your competition.

Why are the reasons customer's leave?

Basically ANY negative experience ANYWHERE in the customer experience opens the door for a loss of a customer. If the customer even thinks that they could do better elsewhere, they will at least check it out. If they feel that doing business at another store will give them greater value, better treatment, fewer problems, more convenience or anything else a customer might value, they will be tempted to check it out.

So streamline your process, address problems proactively and look at every aspect of your business to make it as customer friendly and streamlined as possible. Make doing business with your business and easy and rewarding process. This will help customers stay happy, stay loyal and stay with doing business with your business. Anything short of this is flirting with danger.

21 Give Them More & Charge Them Less

This is a very basic tenant of customer service. Customers will love you whenever you provider a greater value than they expected to get. Any time you can give a customer more and charge them less is a great thing for the customer.

As we stated before, value is more than just price. Value represents price AND any value added extras that your business provides to the customer. Whether that is free services such as delivery, added convenience, better financing or anything else that has value to the customer, these are the things we need to provide to our customers at every opportunity.

Many businesses focus far too much on profit and far too little on providing value. While that might be understandable on one level, it is dangerous on many other levels. While businesses should look for any and all ways to increase profits and their success, they should not always look to accomplish those goals at the expense of the customer. Doing so is a very short sighted view of your business.

Instead, concentrate on providing the very best value you possibly can while still remaining fiscally responsible for the business. This might mean thinking out of the box to establish various value added services and benefits that help you provide greater value without incurring too much additional costs. This can be done if you put your mind to it.

You just have to get in the mindset of the customer, think about what is important to the customer and then make the changes you need to make your business more appealing to the customer. It is that change of attitude that will help you create a better and more desirable business in the eyes of your customers.

22 Take Care of the Little Things!

Contrary to popular belief, most of the largest problems some businesses have today are the result of little things that either went unnoticed or that no one bothered to address because they thought it would make little difference and therefore not worth the effort.

The reality is that most problems DO start out as little things. Little things that would have been easy to address in the beginning but have now grown out of proportion and caused great problems.

Let's say you had one little problem that affected a handful of customers. Not a whole lot of customers but just a few for whatever reason. You decide it either is not worth your time or the expense to make any changes. After all that "little" problem only effects a few people.

But those few people go over to the competition, where that little problem doesn't exist and they like it there. So they spread the word and more people start going to that business. All of a sudden that "little" problem is now a significant or even major problem.

This frequently happens when little things go unaddressed or when we adopt a reactive approach instead of a pro-active one. We should be addressing problems when we are first made aware of them so we catch things early before they effect more customers as time goes on.

In other words, don't ignore the little things. Problems or issues rarely go away without taking any action. If left alone, bad things will grow worse. Without action small problems become big problems. So take care of the little things when you first encounter them and eliminate problems before they start.

This will not only please your customers but also help your business resolve issues with less time, fewer resources and much less stress for both you and your customers.

23   Become the Best
Resource for Your Customers

One thing customers always love is when they have one place they can go to have all their problems resolved. Whether that means having the biggest selection of products to the most complete line of accessories to the most knowledgeable salespeople, what they want is one source for all their needs.

Becoming a single point of resource for customers is one reason why some of the smaller and more specialized stores continue to perform at such a high level today. People go to them instead of the big box stores because at the smaller stores they not only get the products they need but the advice and specialized knowledge they might need as well.

The great thing is that our customers are usually more than willing to pay for that knowledge as well.

They will go to a one stop source and pay slightly higher prices because their time and needs have a certain value to them. So instead of driving around to 7 different places to get accessories, products, advice and other things, they just have one place to go. So instead of spending a half day getting what they need, they spend 30 minutes. This often has tremendous value to most customer.

Becoming a one stop resource does require effort and certain level of commitment. Here are some of the things our customers look for when it comes to their needs:

Product Selection

The problem some stores have is that space is a premium and whenever you try to have everything for everyone, selection often suffers. After all you can only stock as many products as you have room for. So instead of having 6 models of a product you might have one or two. If one of those models is not exactly what the customer wants or needs they might have to settle which does not usually thrill the customer.

But a one stop resource dedicated to a specific type of product might have 6 different manufacturers and 30 different models. Your customers will have a better chance of getting exactly what they want when they need it. In other words, they can count on you for what they need.

Accessories

With some kinds of products, accessories play an important role. If the customer has to go to one place to get the product and somewhere else to get an accessory, they are not going to be happy. But if your store stocks the products and a fairly comprehensive line of accessories, you will not only make your customers happy but you will increase your overall average sale value as well. In other words, if you have it right there on the shelves, your customers will buy more from you.

Knowledgeable Sales People

Big box stores may have friendly people but they might not have the knowledge you need. Sometimes people will switch from department to department so one day they are selling tools and the next day men's clothing. Or turnover is higher in those stores so that once people get actual experience, they leave for a better job. In any case, sales and product knowledge is frequently lacking in some stores.

If your salesmen had in-depth product knowledge and really know the products and what they can and cannot do, that is something of great value for your business and for your customers. Being able to recommend the right product for the right application to the right customer is worth its weight in gold at times.

Practical Experience or Actual Experience

While taking a class or reading the manuals is great for knowing what a product does and how it works, NOTHING beats real-life, on the job learning for the kind of in-depth and practical information that you will never find in a manuals or seminar. What I'm talking about are all the little tips and tricks people get from actually using a piece of equipment or performing a specific task.

Chances are your customers will be coming to you to purchase something that solves a problem or fulfills a specific meal. The more you know about what the customer needs, the better able you will be to help them. If you sell tools and have actually used them on a jobsite, that information might be critical to which products you recommend. If you are a cook and you actually used a mixer or particular oven or other appliance you will be able to advise the customer appropriately.

This kind of knowledge can only be obtained from people who actually have done certain things for a while and know the task or situation inside out. You can learn from their mistakes and their successes thereby shortening the learning curve, and its associated costs, at the same time.

Problem Resolution

You can walk into 1,000 business and find 1,000 sales people who will be more than willing to sell you something. But when you run into a problem, it is amazing how many of those sales people and businesses are nowhere to be found.

Customers with problems need solutions and answers. If you can provide those answers and solutions, or guide to where they can get them, your business will become highly desirable in the community. It seems to be getting harder and harder to find a business that is interested not only in sales but in solving customer problems as well. This is something customers grab hold of when they find it!

After Sales Support and Consultation

Last but certainly not least, if you want to create a loyal customer base, continue to provide everything we have just discussed to your customers after the sale has been completed. It is one thing to solve a problem by selling a customer something. Customers expect that. But when we solve a problem without selling something and do it just to help the customer that makes most people stop and think for a moment.

Becoming known as a community resource for anything takes time and effort.

It requires effort to offer everything a customer needs and it takes a great experience to get those customers to talk about their experience with friends, family and co-workers. But after a while this kind of talk and action takes on a life of its own and begins to steam roll across town. Then you start seeing new people walk through the doors not because of a great sale or your latest advertisement, but for help and assistance and because of your reputation. When you hit this point, you have struck gold.

People sometimes shake their heads as they walk out of a store where they were given help or solutions but not pressured to purchase anything. They wonder why a salesperson or other employee would spend time with them, provide help or assistance, without a sale hanging in the process. After all, when no sale is made, no commissions are earned and no profits generated. So customer wonder why they did it.

Smart employees and business owners understand that a small amount of help or assistance now will help pave the way for sales tomorrow. It is very true that the things we do today help us close sales tomorrow, net month and even next year.

In fact, most customers don't purchase the first time they walk into your store. This is especially true for more expensive purchases. They walk in to see how they are treated and to get a feeling for the type of establishment they are in.

This is one of the customers most vulnerable times. If you can impress them today, you stand a much better chance of selling them products in the future.

Everything we do, every move a business makes and every part of the business is created and built to sell product. But successful businesses understand that in order to sell product you have to give a pretty good reason to the customer to walk through your doors instead of someone else's.

Becoming known as the area's best resource for certain products and services will help you create loyal customers that will love you and help support your business for years to come.

24 Strive to Be the Best

Your business needs to be good. Very good. In fact in some area where competition is especially fierce and cut throat, your business must be better than good. In those situations, your business must be great. It must be the best. It must be the place people in your town talk about when it comes to the products and services you offer.

As we spoke about earlier, there are a lot of people who go through life stating they want to become good at something. While that is admirable, and while many people do achieve that and become good at something, we often need more.

To become successful in life and in business you do not want to set your goal at becoming good at something, you always want to become the best at whatever it is you are trying to learn. There is a very important reason for wanting to be the best and why people with that attitude are often more successful.

That reason is that people who want to be the best try harder, try longer and tend to stay more motivated.

These people are not content to be good at something, they want to be better than anyone else. They want to be better, faster, higher quality and more desirable than any other similar business in town. They don't just want to survive, they want to thrive!

A lot of business owners and employees try like hell to become better at everything they try. They want to make their businesses successful. They want their careers to be successful and they want to experience success in their lives. All that is well and good but people who want to be the best go even further. They drive themselves farther and they don't fall victim to one of the most common problems some people experience every day.

People who strive to be the best never become complacent. They never feel that it is OK to stop learning or improving because they are "good enough". We already mentioned this about how we treat our customers but it should also related to how we structure and run our businesses as well. We should always want to be the best.

The thing about business is that everything is always changing. We might be on top today but someone else makes changes to their business and all of a sudden we are number 2. Not because we got lazy but because we got complacent and stopped trying to always improve.

Every time any of your competition improve and moves forward, if you do nothing you have moved back.

People who demand the best expect the best. They understand that what is the best today will cease to be the best in the future unless they are driven to improve even though they are already the best. When we relax we provide opportunities for others to step in and take what we had built so carefully.

Chances are there are improvements that can be made to your business and your individual efforts. We all tend to get complacent once we experience success. But the difference between truly successful is that they take their current success and they built upon it. They are always looking to make themselves and their business better than anyone else.

When they reach success, they celebrate it and start looking for ways to get to the next level. Their goal is not perfection but rather to always stay one or two steps ahead of everyone else. They do this because they understand that it is always better to be number one than it is to be number two.

So if you are at number one, continue to improve so you can stay number one.

If you are number two or perhaps lower, than see what you can do to improve your business and move up on the chart. Remember you are fighting for customers.

Every little thing you do to make your business better helps your customers at the same time. So if you want to create customers that love you, always keeping trying to be the best at what you do.

Because you deserve the best and so do your customers.

25　Use Problems to Help You Shine!

While nobody likes problems, the fact is that even the best run business, staffed with the best trained and well intentioned people will still generate a problem or two from time to time. So it's not so much whether problems are going to arise but actually when they are going to arise. So it really boils down to what we do and how we react when we do run into a problem.

Despite the very obvious negative aspects of problems, they do give us the opportunity to showcase just how good we can be when it comes to customer service. I know this may sound like a cliché, but under the right circumstances, problems really can be an opportunity for us to create a customer for life.

Anyone can sell a perfect product to the perfect customer at the perfect price at the perfect time and not experience any problems. But even though everything went "perfect" in the customer's mind everything went as expected. You don't buy something expecting to have a problem or you wouldn't buy it in the first place!

But when one of those "perfects" turns out to be not so perfect, we then have the opportunity to step in, resolve the situation and make things right with the customer. When we can successfully resolve a problem for the customer that will create a positive impression in the mind of that customer.

Here's why.

Contrary to what some of your customers might say, most rational people understand that life is not perfect. They all understand that no one is perfect either. (Well some of our customer may think they are perfect but they're really not!) So on one level most customers understand the occasional problem when it happens.

But they also expect that when a problem does pop up, that you will be there to resolve that problem in a timely and appropriate manner. That means supporting the products and services that you sell. As long as you can successfully resolve the situation in such a manner that the customer is satisfied, you could just hit a home run with that customer.

In most cases, here are the things you will have to do when a problem does arise:

Acknowledge the Problem Quickly

When people have a problem they usually want it addressed and resolved as quickly as possible. They don't want to wait days, weeks or months for you to get back to them. They might understand a delay is getting something repaired or replaced but they will not understand with a long delay in initially responding to the problem.

We should aim for a same day response whenever possible. Naturally, if the customer is reporting the problem in person we should have someone there to talk to the customer right then and there. But if it is reported via voice mail or e-mail, same day response is usually always best. Naturally this will depend on what types of products or services you are involved with. Products or services that address critical or health related issues, for example, should probably have a much shorter response time.

The longer we wait to contact the customer the madder they will be and the more time and resources it will take to resolve the problem and satisfy the customer. We need to avoid anything that will make the customer feel worse and strive to make them feel better about you and the situation.

Understand the Expectations of the Customer

Sometimes we have one problem but the customer has their own idea of what needs to happen in order for them to be happy.

We should make every effort to discover what the customer really wants or needs and then try to provide as much of whatever that is to them.

Keep in mind that in order to create a life-long customer we cannot give the customer what they expect, we have to go beyond that. We need to impress them so much that they will remember what happened. Just giving them what they expected will not create that kind of impression or memory.

Always approach problems with a win-win mentality. Go for the resolution that gives the customer the most of what they want while still protecting the interests of the business. If you try to get a win for your business at the expense of the customer, that is going to backfire on you. Always try to give the customer as much of what it is they want whenever possible.

Work with the Customer for a Resolution

Sometimes we have a problem or situation that has more than one possible resolution. When this happens, bring the customer into the process and let them choose which course of action they think is the best one for them. This will help you in two ways.

First, when the customer is involved in the process they will usually be more receptive and pleased with the overall outcome because you made them part of the process used to come up with that outcome. This is not you telling them what is best for them you are allowing them to tell you! It is a subtle difference that usually makes a tremendous difference.

Second, when you make the customer part of the process things tend to go faster, smoother and with overall better results on both sides. You also usually get a final resolution that is better for the customer because only they know what they really want. Allowing the customer to pick the best overall option also relieves some of the pressure off of your shoulders as well.

Take Steps to Insure the Problem Does Not Reoccur

While we said before that no matter what we do, or how hard we try, we are still going to have problems, that doesn't mean we cannot minimize them to the point where real problems are rare. We can help accomplish by following one basic rule. That is that if something happens once, it is likely to happen again unless we do something about it.

When you have a problem don't just resolve it. Instead, dig into it and find out why it happened in the first place. Find out what went wrong and why it went wrong.

Then, once you identified the source of the problem, take steps to fix anything that was wrong, change anything that didn't work and make it much harder for that problem to happen again in the future.

When we take that stances where problems are concerned we not only help the customer with the problem today we also help the customers of the future by removing that problem from happening to them. Though they will never realize it, fixing problems when you first are made aware of them just makes your business more customer friendly and easier to do business with.

Assist the Customer When You Cannot Resolve the Problem

Sometimes there will be problems that we just cannot solve all by ourselves. During those problems we should be doing everything we can do to help the customer get the resolution they deserve.

This might mean providing the homeowner with contact information of the manufacturer or even calling the manufacturer yourself and interceding on behalf of the customer. This can be useful because some manufacturers will listen and do more for a dealer than they would for a single customer.

This also might mean directing the customer to other sources of help or assistance where they can get their problem resolved.

When we take the time and make the effort to help a customer most customers will appreciate it even if they don't show it or say so. But when a customer has a problem they usually feel a little bit helpless and at the mercy of the manufacturer or other party. When they feel that someone wants to help them and actually tries, that impresses them. Again, they might not show it, but later on they will realize it.

Escalate the Problem Whenever Necessary

Unless you are the owner of the business, or unless you have full power to make any and all decisions, there will come times when no matter what you might want to do, you do not have the authority or ability to do so. When this happens you should not just give up and leave the customer with an unresolved problem. Instead you should escalate the situation to someone better able to resolve the issue.

Usually this would be your manager or supervisor but it could also be another department within the company. For example, if someone had a billing problem you might not be able to resolve it personally but you could escalate it to the billing department manager who might be better able to assist the customer.

This is often very effective when a customer wants something far in excess of what they are entitled to or what seems reasonable. We all have our overly demanding customers and escalation is one way of dealing with them. We do the most we can and then we get someone else involved who is better able to determine what the company is willing to do in order to make this customer happy.

Sometimes even escalating the call to a manager is enough to make the customer feel that something is getting done. Just the title of manager suggests more power and a higher level of importance in the mind of the customer. The manager might say the exact same things you had just said but because they are a manager the customer might accept those comments more readily. In that case it is not the person but the title that matters.

26 Give Your Customer's Choices

Here is one tip that can make solving all your problems easier, increase your sales, lower your blood pressure and send you stress level down to the lowest it has been in years! Plus, your customers will usually love it and be far happier in the process! That is where the stress reduction comes in!

When it comes to dealing with customers, most situation go much smoother if you present all the available options to the customer and let them make the final choice or decision on which way to go. This places the customer in the driver's seat and allows them to decide what's best for them.

For example, if a customer wants to purchase a television and you tell him this is the model he wants and then ask him if it will be cash or charge, the customer will likely resist the urge to buy because they are not sure if that really is the model he wants. But if you showed him 3 or 4 different models, explained the differences and allowed him to pick the best one, then the chances of the customer being happy and actually purchasing will go much higher.

Choices also can extend to problem solving as well. You might ask a customer whether he would like a new one or have his existing one repaired. Or whether he would like to exchange his current defective product for the same product or a different model. Here again you are making the customer part of the process.

This tells the customer that you are really concerned that you get what you really want. By allowing the customer to participate in the process you are telling them that this is not about what I want but what you want. In other words, you are telling the customer that their needs matter to you.

The best way to go about this is to provide a few choices to the customer. Not too many because that might just confuse the customer and make it too difficult to make a decision. You don't want him leaving and going home to think about it because you have no idea where he will go once he does make up his mind. You want to give him options now and make it easy for him to decide so he buys now and buys from you.

When it comes to recommendations, it is perfectly fine to recommend one model over another but also make it clear that both or all three models are good choices. Explain the differences and give the customer all the information they need to make the right choices.

Our goals should be to get the customer to purchase the best product for their needs but to purchase it from you and no one else.

When it comes to resolving a problem, sometimes various value added items or services will be part of the resolution. Since we cannot always be sure what value someone might place on something, the best way to go is to present the options or packages and let the customer decide which holds more value for them.

For example, you might say, I can ship the replacement her to the store or deliver it to your home. Which would be more convenient for you? Or, I can either give you the better model for the same price or throw in free delivery. Which would you prefer?

In those examples, you are allowing the customer decide. You are not telling them what you are going to do you are asking them what they want you to do. That can be a big difference. In the first example maybe they are out all day and don't want the product sitting on the front porch where it might get stolen or rained on. In the second example maybe they have a pick-up truck so delivery isn't a big deal but getting the better model really impresses them. Remember it is not the value of something in your mind that matters. It is what the customer thinks that really counts.

Providing choices also helps you decide what is really important to the customer as your conversations move forward. Judging by the choices the customer makes there might be other things you can offer that are similar in nature that might really make the customer happy. Equally important you might realize from their answers things that don't seem to matter at all so you could eliminate those from your offerings.

The great thing about choices is that it gets the customer involved and make them feel part of the process. They are actively involved in how things go and where they end up. Customers who were made part of the process usually are happier and more engaged. They are almost always more satisfied with the outcome than those who think they were dictated to throughout the process.

27   Show them Appreciation

Everyone likes to feel appreciated and customers are certainly no different. But in order to feel appreciated they have to know they are appreciated. That part of the process is up to the business and its employees.

When it comes to showing your customers how much you appreciate them, here are a few of the most common ways businesses show their appreciation:

Customer Rewards

We all have a wallet full of customer loyalty cards that we use to get lower prices, earn points towards free products or services and other programs that provide us with benefits for shopping at the same store. These cards allow the business to give back something to their customers for their continued patronage. You would be surprised how much these influence where people shop!

Another benefit of these programs is that you usually have to sign up for them which means capturing the customer's name, address, phone number and sometimes e-mail.

This allows you to create special customer sales and awards as well as a marketing list.

Free Gifts

Everyone likes to get free stuff and customers are no different. If you send your customer a coupon for a free service or product as a thank you for their past business, customers will love you! Just make the free product something that people really want and not a piece of crap you can't sell and want to get rid of.

Some businesses use these free gift offers as a way to get the customer into their store in the hope that they will purchase more products during their visit. For example you might offer a customer a free loaf of bread and then they wind up buying their milk eggs and other groceries while they are there.

Restaurants use this as well when they offer their customers a free entrée when they buy one. They do this because they know they will sell at least two drinks and maybe a couple of appetizers and desserts as well. But the customer doesn't think about this because all they know is that they scored a free entrée! So where do you think they will go out to dinner next???

Special Sales

Whenever you can give your customers a better price on something they need, you will make them happy. Offering special "member's only" sales to your existing customers not only increase your current sales you are thanking your customers for their past purchases! This is the very definition of a win-win!

Community Involvement

Many customers love the community is which they live. When they see a business giving back to the community in thanking their customers for their business, it makes the business more desirable in the eyes of the customers. There is a part of their brain that says that since you gave back to us we should continue to do business with you. You appreciate us and we appreciate you.

Sponsor a local event, a sports team or a scout troop. Get your name out there and make it known that you support the community. The cost isn't all that high and it might generate customer good will and sales like no paid advertisement ever could!

Telling Them

Sometimes the best ways are the easiest ways. If you really appreciate a customer's business, why not take a moment and just tell them face to face?

This will really impress most customers if you do it right and are sincere. Saying something like "Mr. Bila, thank you for your purchase. I know you have been coming here for a long time and I want you to know we appreciate you and your business" will resonate with the customer and make him feel good about where he does business.

Holiday or Birthday Cards

If you sell high end or expensive products you might want to consider sending our holiday or birthday cards to your customers. These are nice little reminders that someone was thinking about you and values your business.

You might even include a birthday coupon with a discount or free product to help you celebrate your birthday. While it is the thought that counts, a little bonus is never a bad thing!

28 Always Have What Your Customers Want

You can have the best run business with the friendliest and most helpful employees but if you don't have what you customer wants when they want it, you are not likely to be a hit with your customer.

Your customers expect you to have the products and services they need when they walk through the door. If you don't have them, they will look somewhere else. Whenever you make them look somewhere else, you are giving an opportunity to your competition to take that customer away from you. That can be dangerous.

But always having what your customer wants takes time, money and experience. It also requires an in-depth knowledge of both your products and customer base. In other words, you have to understand what your customer wants, why they want it and what products will best suit their needs.

But even if you have the right products, you also have to have the right quantities of those products so they are in stock and ready for purchase when the customer wants them. The best selection at the lowest prices means absolutely nothing if you don't have what they need in stock. If you are out of stock your customer is not likely to wait if there are alternatives. They will go somewhere else and you know where that goes!

That means having adequate stock especially on sale or advertised items. When you advertise something at a lower price and then don't have it, your customers might think you are trying to cheat them even if that is not the case. Remember, perception is everything and if the customer thinks you are cheating them, then in their mind you are cheating them.

Another thing that separates great businesses from the rest of the competition is something you rarely see any more. I'm not sure why that is except for the fact that it is so hard to keep a huge selection with a wide range of variety these days. But the great businesses do one thing that the rest don't. They listen to their customers and they bring in the products their customers ask for.

For example, if a customer comes in and asks for something they don't carry or sell, they make a note of it.

If it makes sense to carry that product, or if the request is made by several customers, then they bring it in and stock it in the store. This is an excellent way to determine what you sell. It is far better than the recommendation of the manufacturer's rep who just wants you to but more of everything he or she sells. These are products you know already have a market in your area. If you don't sell them someone else will.

Hearing and making note of what your customers want allows you to become more responsive and to increase your chances of having what your customers want when they want it. Stock is one thing that often avoids scrutiny when it comes to customer service. But the fact remains.

If you don't have what your customers need or want, they will go somewhere else.

30 Sell Them More Stuff!

This one might surprise you but you can really make a customer love you by selling them more products. We accomplish this by not trying to sell them things they don't need or by badgering them with high pressure sales pitches. Instead, we try and make sure they have everything they need to complete their purchase or might need to get the full benefits from their products.

Have you ever come home after buying something, unpacked your purchase and then realized that you needed something else in order for you to use your new purchase? Maybe you need batteries or a cable or some accessory that you weren't aware of. We have all had that experience.

How did that make you feel? Were you happy with your purchase and the store where you bought it or were you annoyed because the store didn't make you aware of the things that were not included so you could buy them right then and there if you needed them?

These are called add-on sales and they do more than make customers happy. They also increase the amount of many sales and therefore bring in more revenue from the same customer! This results in higher profits with less advertising expenses.

These sales are easier because you already have conquered the barrier of the customer not feeling secure enough to make their purchase from you. After all, the customer was already willing to purchase their primary product so that means they are open to doing business from you. So with that barrier knocked down, the rest of the sales process becomes much easier.

The logical process when it comes to add-on sales is to start with needed accessories that are not included with the main product. The usually items like this are batteries, cases, cables and other similar items. These are the things you MUST have to use what you just bought.

The second group are accessories that are available for what you purchased. These accessories might enable the product to do more or handle different tasks or even give you the ability to plug the product in instead of using batteries. These are the products you don't NEED to use the product but might want based on your situation.

For example, if you purchase a power saw, you might suggest different types of blades so you can cut different materials.

If, during the initial sales process, your customer asked for a saw that could cut metal, then the ideal accessory would be the blade you would use to cut metal. When you suggest these items you are not just selling the customer something more, you are making sure they will be able to do what they need to do immediately when they get home.

The last group of items might be add-on items like service contracts, fabric protection plans, protection products like screen protectors, lighting and other items. These are the products you sell that COMPLIMENT the products the customers are going to purchase.

All of those items share one very important thing. They are all directly related to the product the customer is already going to buy. These are things the customer could legitimately need to either use or get more enjoyment or function from their purchase. In other words, they help make the original purchase better and more efficient.

These purchases increase the likelihood that the customer ill have everything they need when they get home and will not have to get back in the car to get batteries or cables or anything else. When salesmen cover these kinds of purchases they are doing their customers a favor because they are providing an important service.

These are NOT products or items that we just try to sell the customer just to make a sale. We don't go to a customer and say something like "That's a nice television you are purchasing there. How about a set of kitchen pots to go with it?" That is the type of sales approach customers don't like.

Another potential problem appears when the salesman tries to sell too many things to the customer. S and a connection cable. But if you go down a list and ask the customer if they need 47 different accessories, that is going too far. You need to develop a balances between trying to increase the sale and helping the customer and offering too many products and annoying the customer. You can generally tell from the facial expression or behavior of the customer when they start to get tired of being asked to purchase things.

Try and think about what the customer will need to get the most use from their current purchase. Then, if there are complementary products that will benefit your customer, recommend them. You just might become the hero because you will save them a trip to the store to get what they should have had in the first place!

30 Request Feedback

We saved the most important item for last because this particular item is the most important thing you can do when it comes to creating the very best customer experience and having your customers fall in love with you and your business. Even though some of the tips you have read so far touched on this, it bears repeating in a more in-depth manner. So we decided to finish this book with this one directive.

Solicit feedback from your customers. Not just after their purchase but during the sales or customer service process. Ask them for their opinions or feelings about how things are going. Ask them what they feel should happen or why they came in your store in the first place. Ask them what they need and ask them how you can help them.

In other words, ask customers. Ask questions designed to solicit answers to things you either don't know or aren't sure of. Your questions should either provide you with specific answers or clarification of something that is vague.

You want to get as much information as you can in order to make the best decisions and take the best approach.

Ask people when they walk through the door if you can help them? Don't wait for them to approach you because some of your customers might never do that. Make the first move and make it easy for them to talk to you.

If people look like they need help, offer it. Ask them how you can help them. Find out what they want or what problem they are looking to solve. Sometimes it is obvious while other times it just isn't.

If you are at the exits or if you are a cashier, ask the customer if they found everything they were looking for or if you can help them with anything else. This will enable you to salvage a possible lost sale or make an existing sale larger. Any unaddressed need will make the customer unhappy and might negatively impact their overall experience.

If the purchase was a large or expensive item, wait a few days and call the customer to make sure they are happy and have not experienced any problems. Many businesses shy away from this because during some of those calls they might uncover a problem and then have to deal with it and resolve it. Or, they may uncover a very demanding customer and the additional call might create issues.

But in each of these examples where we ask questions we are just asking for feedback from our customers. We are asking them for their thoughts and opinions as well as for specific information that might only be relevant to them. Feedback of any kind can prove invaluable because it gives us more fact and fewer assumptions.

Feedback is also the only really accurate way we can use to find out exactly what our customers think about us and our business. Even though some of the comments are bound to be negative or at least criticisms, these comments give us an inside look at what our customers are thinking about us. This gives us an idea about what needs to be changed or possibly even eliminated.

By finding out what people like and dislike about us, we can take steps to give them more of what they like while limiting what they don't like. This is the way businesses transform them from owner driven businesses to customer driven businesses.

Successful businesses rarely are built overnight. No matter how perceptive we try to be and no matter how hard we try to look at things from the customer perspective, there will always be things we will miss. Even the things we got right in the beginning eventually will get outdated as our competition makes their businesses different.

What this all boils down to is that every business must constantly change in order to become great and remain great. Nothing in this world stays the same and neither can your business. By getting feedback from our customers we can make changes now before they become necessary so we will always be constantly moving forward and never staying the same or moving backwards.

This is important because a large number of customers are extremely fickle. They will love you to death today until your competition lowers their prices or improves their service. Then they are out the door and doing business with them! But by always staying ahead of everyone else and by always being the best, you never give anyone a reason to even think about looking elsewhere.

So let's develop a plan that will provide us with the customer feedback we need to always be aware and responsive to our customer's needs. It's not hard, it's not expensive and it really needs to be done. So let's just do it. And do it now.

Conclusion

Well, hopefully by now you have a better idea on what you can do to create a much better customer experience for all your customers. You also know why you should become more customer focused so you can give your customers more of what they want or need. If you have changed your attitude regarding your customers and their customer experience, then we have accomplished our main goal.

But before we finish, let me share one more important thing with you. When it comes to everything in this book, and your customer's experience, you must be sincere in your efforts. If you are doing something strictly to make more sales and generate more profits, your customers will see right through you. They will understand why you are doing things and your efforts will not have the same effect. But the great thing is that if you are sincere when it comes to the things in this book that you are going to do, you WILL increase sales, profits and the growth of your business.

One of the greatest things about doing this is because in the world we live in there are so many businesses who don't bother to do these things. For every business that doesn't take their customers seriously, there is an opportunity for a business such as yours to come in and grab more customers. All you need to do is provide a better overall value and customer experience and you won't have to go out and find customers because pretty soon those customers are going to come looking for you!

Another great thing to remember is that everything we covered in this book presents a win-win for you and your business and the customer. That means both you and your customer will reap benefits from your efforts. This is just not providing more for the customer. It is providing more for the customer and getting more from the customer in return.

So now that you have the knowledge and hopefully a few ideas, you have a decision to make. You can continue what you are doing and hope that it continues to work for you or you can take action. Taking action will help you change. After all if you change nothing, nothing changes.

So pick one or two things from this book and figure out how to implement them in your business. Then, make sure your employees read this book as well so they can create the same customer focused attitude that you now have.

That is another win-win we can all embrace.

For More Books on

Customer Service Training,

Please go to our Website at:

http://www.infowhse.com

Be sure to visit our site and
sign up for our mailing list for
more great information, special
offers and other FREE benefits!

It's FREE!